ONLY IN DARKNESS CAN YOU SEE THE STARS

MARTIN LUTHER KING JR

SANTOSH BAKAYA

Vitasta
LET KNOWLEDGE SPREAD

Published by
Renu Kaul Verma
Vitasta Publishing Pvt Ltd
2/15, Ansari Road, Daryaganj
New Delhi - 110 002
info@vitastapublishing.com

ISBN 978-93-86473-62-2

First Edition 2019
MRP ₹ 495

This book contains educational content for India. The photographs of Martin Luther King Jr are from Open Source and the publisher acknowledges the various oganisations to which they are copyrighted.

Cover and layout by Somesh Kumar Mishra
Printed by Vikas Computer and Printers

Contents

My mother bore me in the Southern wild,
And I am black, but O! my soul is white;
White as an angel is the English child:
But I am black as if bereaved of light.
My mother taught me underneath a tree
And sitting down before the heat of day,
She took me on her lap and kissed me,
And pointed to the east, began to say.
Look on the rising sun: there God does live
And gives his light, and gives his heat away.
And flowers and trees and beasts and men receive,
Comfort in morning joy in the noonday.
And we are put on earth a little space,
That we may learn to bear the beams of love,
And these black bodies and this sun burnt face
Is but a cloud, and like a shady grove.
For when our souls have learn'd the heat to bear
The cloud will vanish we shall hear his voice.
Saying: come out from the grove, my love and care,
And round my golden tent like lambs rejoice.
Thus did my mother say and kissed me,
And thus I say to little English boy.
When I from black and he from white cloud free,
And around the test of God like lambs we joy.

I'll shade him from the heat till he can bear,
To lean in joy upon our father's knee.
And then I'll stand and stroke his silver hair,
And be like him and then he will love me.

—From *The Little Black Boy* by William Blake

The homes of many of us have been destroyed, and the lives of young and old have been taken. There's scarcely a household that hasn't been struck to the heart. And why? Surely you must have asked yourselves this question? Why in all conscience should these be the ones to suffer, children, old people, a young girl at the height of her loveliness, why these? Are these our soldiers? Are these our fighters? Why should they be sacrificed?

—The Vicar speaking at the badly damaged church in *Mrs Miniver*
– the 1942 Academy award winning film

Gandhi was probably the first person in history to lift the love ethic of Jesus above mere interaction between individuals to a powerful and effective social force on a large scale.

— Martin Luther King Jr

Too bad, you say, that Martin Luther King Jr died so young. I feel that way too. But, as I have said many times before, it isn't how long one lives, but how well; it's what one accomplishes for mankind that matters. Jesus died at 33; Joan of Arc at 19; Byron and Burns at 36, Keats at 25; Marlow at 29; Shelley at 30; Dunbar before 35; John Fitzgerald Kennedy at 46; William Rainey Harper at 49; and Martin Luther King Jr at 39.

—Benjamin E May Delivering King's eulogy at Morehouse
on 9 April 1968

Everybody can be great... because anybody can serve. You don't have to have a college degree to serve, you don't have to make your subject and your verb agree to serve, you don't have to know about Plato and Aristotle to serve, you don't have to know Einstein's theory of relativity to serve, you don't have to know the second theory of thermodynamics in physics to serve, you only need a heart full of grace, a soul generated by love, and you can be that servant.'

— Martin Luther King Jr

—The Drum Major Instinct – Ebenezer Baptist Church, Atlanta, GA, 4 February 1968

Author's Note

It was the month of February 2005, the news about the re-enactment of Dandi March was very much in the air, and I was talking to my undergraduate students about the *half-naked fakir*'s role in the national movement, when a chit of a boy shot up to his full height of five feet nothing, and seething with indignation, retorted:

'Madam, he was responsible for the partition of India.'

What the tiny boy lacked in height, he tried to make up by his indignant squeals of disagreement.

'Was he? Where did you read that?', I asked.

'Well ...!'

'Before criticising anyone, you should at least read about the person and then argue.'

'Madam, where is the question of reading? It's a universal truth. Everyone knows that he was the villain of the piece', another boy remarked with a cocky air.

'Yes, it's a well-known fact', still another boy rejoined, almost stumbling under the weight of his swaggering confidence.

'Do you know that Gandhi was a sad man when India was partitioned – and he regarded partition as a disaster?

Mohammad Ali Jinnah had an iron resolve to father Pakistan, and Gandhi was not in a position to dilute this resolution.'

'Do you know that when India was celebrating Independence Day on 15 August 1947, Gandhi was not part of the celebration? He was spending the day in a broken-down house in Calcutta among filth and broken glass.'

My words were having no effect on the forty odd students who sat before me, with '*we know better than you*' expressions on their faces, shining with a misplaced confidence. Not even thin slivers of facts could slip through their minds.

'Madam, the need of the hour is a Hitler, not a Gandhi.'

'Gandhi is long dead – why revive him?'

'Truth and non-violence have lost their relevance.'

'My favourite book is "Mein Kamph" and not "My Experiments with Truth."'

'Have you read any of the two?'

'I haven't read them, but Hitler was a great man – a brave man so …'

'But he killed so many Jews. How do you justify that?', I stuttered, agonised.

'Karna Padta Hai' (one has to do it) squealed the tiny one with quadrupled vigor.

'Rashtra Ko Strong Banane Ke Liye Yeh Bhi Karna Padta Hai' (one has to do such things to strengthen the nation) remarked the cocky boy becoming cockier.

All these remarks whirled around, like dark and malevolent clouds threatening to engulf me. Before these clouds could totally drown me, I stumbled out of the classroom, totally disheartened, disillusioned and sad.

Every cloud has a silver lining, they say, but there appeared no redeeming feature in these sinister clouds. I felt hopelessly lost, the silver lining totally eluding me.

It was the first week of December 2008. People throughout the country were still recovering from the aftershocks of the Mumbai 26/11 terrorist attack, the bloodiest terror attack in the country, the echoes of the blast still ringing in their ears. I sat all alone in my class room, waiting for my final year post-graduate students to turn up, with Martin Luther King (MLK) Jr's words persistently ringing in my ears, 'over the bleached bones and jumbled residues of numerous civilisations are written the pathetic words: Too late … we still have a choice today, nonviolent co-existence or violent co-annihilation', when a student walked up to me with diffident steps, holding something in his hand.

'Could you tell us something about this?' He asked. In his outstretched hand was a paper clipping regarding the significance of MLK Jr's, *I have a dream* speech and his comparison with Gandhi.

The boy was the same chit of a boy who had cried himself hoarse condemning Gandhi and his creed of non-violence just three years back, when he was a second year undergraduate student.

He shot out many questions, one after the other:

'This was his most famous speech, wasn't it?'

'He was a great, orator, wasn't he?'

'Where can we hear his speeches?'

'Who killed him?'

'Why was he killed?'

'Why do people kill?'

'In the present strife-torn world, we need men like Gandhi and King, don't we, madam?'

Soon the classroom was full of boys and girls hurling their queries at me.

Miles away, a man was on the verge of taking oath as the first black President to adorn the White House, realising Martin Luther King Jr's dream that someday there would surely dawn a day in America, when people would be known 'not by the colour of their skin, but by the content of their character'. That day was just round the corner.

I beamed at the class and smiled at the wisp of a boy, who appeared to have gained a couple of inches in the past three years. He looked taller. The menacing clouds which had threatened to engulf me not long back were still there, but I am positive that I saw a silver lining surrounding them.

'You know, one of my favourite films is *The Green Mile*. I saw it long back, but something which one of the characters, a gentle giant, John Coffey, who is in death row for a crime which he did not commit, says, remained etched in my mind.'

'What did he say?' The class was all agog.

'Mostly I'm tired of people being ugly to each other. I'm tired of all the pain I feel and hear in the world every day. There's too much of it. It's like pieces of glass in my head.'

'Yes, why be ugly to each other? That is exactly what King was fighting against. That is what Gandhi was fighting against. King talked of a kind of "dangerous unselfishness."'

'With violence all round us, it is high time we made non-violence the rallying cry, otherwise we will be left with nothing else but bleached bones and jumbled remains.

The students looked at me, slow comprehension dawning, and as I left the class, I could feel (maybe it was a wishful thinking) the veil of mist surrounding them slowly evanescing.

Acknowledgements

It was a day in the year 2012, and my daughter was in the twelfth standard. '*Come listen to this*,' I yelled to her when she entered the room.

She did come, but did not listen, her eyes squinty, nostrils flared. 'Oh, mom, I have no time.' She said dismissively.

'But, this is a famous speech; you will be mesmerised by the voice,' I said, eyes still riveted on the computer screen and ears listening to the rhythmic cadences of that famous voice.

'Aw, come on, mom,' she said, hardly interested in what I had to say, and flounced out of the room.

A trifle disappointed, I went back to the computer screen, Martin Luther King's words pouring forth with a passionate intensity:

'With this faith, we will be able to transform the jangling discords of our nation into a beautiful symphony of brotherhood.'

A couple of days later, when she returned from school, she flung her satchel on the settee, and said, 'There is a declamation contest in school. I want to participate. May I deliver that speech of Martin Luther King Jr, "I Have a Dream", the one you were listening to the other day?' She asked.

I looked at her with a new interest. 'Oh, that's fine. Come on, let's listen to it again', I said enthusiastically.

'Do you think I will be able to speak? He is so awesome', she said diffidently.

'Oh, don't worry. He is indeed awesome, but, believe me, you will be brilliant', I reassured her.

After the contest, she came home, not exactly crestfallen, but quite morose for not having won a prize. 'Don't worry, mom, I have a dream that one day …', she remarked and once again flounced off.

It was during those days that my daughter had been truly initiated into the dream of Martin Luther King Jr Later, she wanted to know more and still more about this passionate and awe-inspiring dreamer, with the result that soon she got absolutely hooked on to Martin Luther King Jr's dream and his ideology of nonviolence.

'Mom, in India, not many know about Martin Luther King Jr, why don't you write his biography?'

'There are so many biographies on him, why will they read mine?'

'You will know only when you write', she said, with a matter-of-fact air and once again hopped out of the room.

I completed writing this biography a couple of years back, but, it continued gathering dust for many years and Renu Kaul Verma, who had bulldozed me into completing my *Ballad of Bapu* (my poetic biography of Mahatma Gandhi, 2015) again appeared on the scene, asking me to finish it. And I did!

So this book would not have been possible without the

gentle reminders and the subtle prodding of Renu Kaul Verma, the dynamic CEO of Vitasta Publishing. Hence, my big thanks to her for making this dream happen, thanks a lot to my editor Papri Sri Raman who has done a commendable job, and to my daughter who planted the dream in my mind.

I also wish to thank Lalit, my husband, who has always smiled beatifically at my creative tantrums, with what looks like exemplary equanimity, but is actually a well-masked, white-knuckled-intensity of apprehension (what next?), when I have thrust my so-called creative pieces at him.

My warm gratitude to Dr Ampat Koshy for subtly bulldozing me and not allowing me to luxuriate in the pleasures of procrastination.

A writer needs readers who cheer and applaud, so I would like to thank all my friends and regular readers in The Significant League who have unfailingly read whatever I have penned.

The Author and Publisher also thank the American Centre, New Delhi for photographs of the Kings' visit to India which has enriched this edition.

Prologue

On 4 April 1968, at 5 pm, Rev Samuel 'Billy' Kyles arrived at Lorraine Motel to pick up his friends. Ralph Abernathy, he and Martin Luther King indulged in a light-hearted banter and some back-slapping bonhomie, while the outside world perhaps wondered what these three preachers were doing in a room for an hour.

Later, Abernathy went into the bathroom to shave and Kyles, asking everyone to hurry up, hastened out of the room, to his car.

'Guys, come on, we have a rally tonight, let's go', Rev Kyles said to Jackson and King, as he headed towards the stairs.

Kyles had bought a new house in 1968, and he was honoured that King planned to dine with him. Tongue in cheek, King quipped, 'If I go to your house and I discover that you bought a house and can't buy food, I'm gonna call all the TV and radio stations and tell them Kyles bought a house, but he can't buy food.'

Kyles started down the stairs. He had hardly walked five or six steps, when a shot rang out. It was 6.01 pm.

Was it a car backfire?

'Take cover,' King's assistants shouted from down below, some hiding behind cars and some falling to the pavement.

Martin Luther King Jr, who, just a day before had talked of difficult times ahead, had also hoped for a long life and in the same breath, had pointed out, '… I've seen the Promised Land. I may not go there with you', was now lying down on the concrete floor of the balcony, with a huge wound covering his right jaw, definitely not in a position 'to go there' with his beloved brethren, his brethren who had straightened their backs, and were now yearning to be absolutely free.

'Martin, it's all right. Don't worry, this is Ralph. This is Ralph', an utterly devastated Ralph Abernathy cradled his head, caressing the left side of his jaw, while a man who turned out to be an undercover police man, Marrell Mccollough, tried to dab at the wound with a towel.

But nothing was all right. Though conscious, King couldn't speak. There was chaotic confusion all around, people down below were milling around in the dark – groaning, crying and screaming.

A thunderstruck Andrew Young ran up the stairs, and throwing himself on King, started looking frantically for the pulse. Unable to find it, he burst into sobs, crying, 'Oh my God, it's all over.'

'No, it's not over, don't you ever say that', Abernathy spoke through tears.

By now, Hosea Williams, Jesse Jackson and Bernard Lee had also rushed up the stairs. A photographer, James Louis, captured certain moments of the scene, especially of Andrew Young and others frantically pointing towards some derelict buildings located on Mulberry Street, the direction from which the gunshots appeared to have been fired.

Within no time, policemen had converged on the scene. An ambulance also arrived, and the stretcher bearers carried King away. An absolutely dazed Ralph who had refused to leave the side of his 'buddy', also climbed into the ambulance, which dashed towards St Joseph's Hospital.

Martin Luther King Jr, who had helped straighten the backs of his brethren, who had tried to resuscitate a comatose nation, who had been undeterred by Bull Connor's dogs and high-powered water hoses, just the other day, talking of a certain kind of fire that no water could put out, was now lying inert on a table in the brightly lit emergency room – his dream shattered, his fire extinguished, and his back broken. Abernathy and Bernard Lee, who hovered around him, refused to move, even when a nurse asked them to leave.

While a team of doctors worked frantically on him, massaging him and attending to his wounds, Lee and Abernathy stood against the wall – in their own cocoon of grief, silently praying for their friend. With a stab of anguish, Abernathy realised that his friend was beyond all hope and prayers. He had noticed a huge hole in his body, which no prayer could fill. The pulse monitor above the operating table was hardly registering a signal.

Martin Luther King Jr was slowly but surely slipping into eternal sleep. There was darkness all around and despite his recent pronouncement – that only when it is dark enough, can one see the stars – his friends could see only an all-enveloping darkness around them, their friend yearning to be free – free of all earthly shackles, of all earthly attachments.

The dreamer was on the verge of unleashing a horrendous nightmare on his family, his friends, his people and his nation.

And then it was all over in a moment on 9 April 1968. The time was 7.05 pm.

At the funeral service, at Ebenezer Baptist Church, where both father and son had served as pastors, there was a massive turnout.

As Alfred Daniel Williams King ('AD'), his younger brother, tried to wipe his tears and Martin's wife, Coretta, sat in sad elegance, the senior Kings bowed down under the burden of grief, the King children too small to understand the colossal loss that they had suffered, suddenly his deep and beautifully modulated voice echoed in the quiet confines of the church. A disembodied voice which had delivered a historic sermon on 4 February 1968, just two months before, in the same church, giving a new definition of greatness:

'You don't have to have a college degree to serve, you don't have to make your subject and your verb agree to serve, you don't have to know about Plato and Aristotle to serve, you don't have to know Einstein's Theory of Relativity to serve, you don't have to know the second theory of thermodynamics in physics to serve, you only need a heart full of grace, a soul generated by love, and you can be that servant.'

The 'heart full of grace' had stopped beating and his family was devastated. Was her beloved husband really no more? An utterly distraught Coretta asked herself. Would they never ever see their beloved son again, the senior Kings thought, with a stab of anguish, while the children hoped that their father would suddenly appear before them and everything would be alright. Bernice, the youngest child, only five, sat in her mother's lap, looking around dazedly, wondering how she could still hear her beloved dad's voice, if he was no more.

As thoughts churned in their minds, the voice went on:

'I'd like somebody to mention that day that Martin Luther King Jr tried to give his life serving others.'

... tried to love somebody,

... tried to be right on the war question,

... did try to feed the hungry,

... to clothe those who were naked,

… tried in my life to visit those who were in prison,
… tried to love and serve humanity.

The recorded voice reverberated in the hall, and the senior Kings closed their tear-filled eyes, as splintered chunks of memory, shards of nostalgia poked them from all directions, forming a crazy collage of tinker toys, juvenile pranks, grins, giggles and guffaws, sibling rivalry, storytelling sessions, music lessons, parental reprimands and childish escapades in 501, Auburn Avenue …

And a happy but cloudy day, just 39 years ago, when a reluctant son had ripped apart the clouds of uncertainty with a delayed lusty roar to be born into an unjust world.

THE EARLY YEARS

ON 15 JANUARY 1929, a little after noon, brooding clouds hung low on this cold Saturday, keenly watching over the birth of a black child in White America.

Yes, it was no big deal, as there was no dearth of black children in White America – nameless children who were called *niggers* – children who grew up to be big men, but were still called 'boys' – little bewildered children who were called 'dirty and ignorant' and shunned by white mothers – children who could not visit certain places merely because they were coloured differently – children who suffered repeated indignities and abuses while riding on segregated buses, along with their parents, who were known 'by the colour of their skin rather than by the content of their character' – children who wondered why certain restaurants and stores did not welcome them – children who suffered bitter stings of discrimination and shed impotent tears in the seclusion of their dark and desolate ghettos, wondering why, why, why; weren't all men and women equal?

'No', they were told. It was the rule and one had to follows rules.

Black children who grew up and proclaimed, like the nameless black protagonist in Ralph Ellison's great novel, *Invisible Man* (1972), that they were invisible simply because people refused to see them.

Black children, who did not know the meaning of the Emancipation Proclamation, tried to gauge the meaning of the rampant injustice and hate.

Children who tried in vain to fight the negative stereotypes which were derisively called their natural characteristics.

Children, who like '*the little black boy*' of William Blake, moaned, 'And I am black, but O! My soul is white.'

Children, who looked at the 'White' and 'Coloured' signs on rest room doors, asked their parents 'why?'

Children, who surreptitiously bleached themselves white, in the juvenile hope to be more socially acceptable to the whites.

This little black child would one day mesmerise the world

Many changed the colour of their skin,
like the famous singer and dancer Michael Jackson.

with his powerful baritone, setting rural Negro Baptists in Georgia to rhythmically respond to words like, 'The cloud is dark but the sun is shining on the other side', filling New York's Riverside Church with eloquence about the 'battering rams of historical necessity', hushing the crowd with his famous words, 'Five score years ago, a great American in whose symbolic shadow we stand today, signed the Emancipation Proclamation ... but one hundred years later, the Negro is still not free.'

But that day, he lay uncannily quiet in his crib. For a moment, Dr Charles Johnson feared him to be stillborn and spanked him several times before he cried. Was something wrong with him?

Nothing was wrong with him, but everything was wrong with the world he was born into.

He was probably weighing the pros and cons of making his entry into the big, bad world, where hate, bigotry and injustice reigned supreme, perhaps bracing himself up for the bitter stings of discrimination, which he would have to face in the white dominated world, perhaps collecting his resources to face the insults and iniquities of an unjust world? This poor little black child almost smothered and had to be spanked repeatedly before he showed any signs of life.

Daddy King, who was still a student at Morehouse College and pastor of two small churches in the city, was so excited at this news that he jumped up to touch the ceiling in the hallway outside the bedroom where his firstborn son had slowly but surely stirred back to life.

His home at 501 Auburn Avenue burst into spontaneous joy.

Sixteen months prior to Martin's birth, sister Christine had been born, in September 1927. His younger brother, AD, named after his maternal grandfather, Alfred Daniel Williams would be born eighteen months later in 1931.*

Together, the three of them, like all normal children, got into trouble, were involved in many an escapade and a scuffle, often falling victims to sibling rivalry.

Once, they locked themselves in the hall cabinet, almost breaking it. Many a time, he would be so engrossed in chasing a ball, or riding a bicycle on the street, that he would be happily unaware of a speeding car. One day, he was clubbed on his head by AD with a baseball bat, who, as their father conceded, could be 'a little rough at times', and 'let his toughness build a reputation throughout our neighbourhood (King Sr 126)'.

Mrs King later recalled that her kids often brought so many other children into the yard that she was often asked if she was running a playground. She remembered how he always wanted to do things differently and that he eventually did manage to do it his way.[1]

'Mama' and 'Mother Dear', these two maternal figures had a profoundly lasting influence on young Martin. Grandmother Williams or Mama, who excelled as a storyteller regaled the children with Biblical stories and as young Martin headed

* Like his brother, a staunch believer in the significance of nonviolence, AD was also deeply involved in the civil rights movement, but was content to bask in the reflected glory of his famous brother. After his brother's assassination, speculation was rife that he might take over the mantle of his brother as the president of the Southern Christian Leadership Conference, SCLC, but he did not appear to be keen, although he continued to work for the SCLC Pastor at Zion Baptist Church, Louisville, Kentucky, in 1965. After his brother's death, he returned to Ebenezer Baptist Church where he had been earlier assisting his father. In September 1968, he became the co-pastor. On 21 July 1969, at the age of 39, he was found dead in the pool at his home. Although shrouded in controversy, the cause of his death was stated as accidental drowning.

towards manhood, these stories, related by his 'saintly' Mama, never left his heart and mind.

Daddy King wanted the firstborn to be named after him. Since his mother's name for him was Mike, the doctor entered the name 'Michael King Jr' on the little boy's birth certificate. It was only in 1934, the year young Martin joined the church, that Daddy King officially corrected their names to Martin Luther King Sr and Martin Luther King Jr But Mike was still the name Daddy King went by, and Martin was the name for the junior.

Auburn Avenue, built in 1895, was known as the Williams House after Martin's maternal grandfather, Rev AD Williams. It was a block away from Ebenezer Baptist Church where Rev Williams was pastor. Rev Williams and his wife, Jennie, bought the house in 1909.

In 1926, after his marriage to Alberta, the Williams' only daughter, Martin Luther King Sr (known then as Michael King) moved into his in-law's house, and it was here that the three King children were born – Christine in 1927, Martin in 1929 and AD (Alfred Daniel) in 1930.

Love, compassion, courtesy, hard work, dignity abounded in this thirteen-room snug house, where young Martin always tried to prove his one-up-man-ship over his older sister, Christine, with whom his relationship was marked by a fierce academic competition.

Protected from the spine-chilling blights of discrimination, and economic deprivation, the Kings and their neighbours were successful middle class professionals and businessmen – a far cry from the poor blacks in Atlanta's ghettos, who were financially deprived, psychologically battered, and often physically assaulted.

Cocooned by the warm affection of parents and grandparents, young Martin played many a game on King's Street, *Sweet Auburn*, and many a prank along with his siblings. He had a normal and typical boyhood of his time. The kids were quizzed on politics at the dinner table by Daddy King, while their mother, who had a passion for music, held rehearsals for the Ebenezer Baptist Church Choir. She even hired a music teacher to give the children music lessons. Martin did not

King Sr, flanked by wife Alberta and mother-in-law, Jeanne C Parks and three King children, Martin Luther Jr at the right.

go beyond memorising the first few measures of Beethoven's *Moonlight Sonata*.

Like all brothers, in bouts of juvenile glee, Martin loved to torture Christine by destroying her dolls and, scattering the pieces all around the house, to their mother's absolute chagrin.

Surrounded by Tinker toys, marbles, Lincoln Logs and other toys, young Martin impishly shirked the household chores assigned to him, invariably scurrying to the washroom when it was his turn to wash the dishes.

A spring Sunday in 1934

Ebenezer Baptist Church was bursting with men, women and children clothed in their Sunday best. It was the middle of a spring revival and a guest evangelist had come from Virginia. Martin sat in the King family pew with Mama and Christine. Daddy King adorned the pastor's chair, while Mother Dear sat at the piano, near the singing choir.

The evangelist exhorted the people to join the church and six-year-old Christine made a dash for the pulpit, the first to offer a pledge that morning.

How could Christine get ahead of him? So, five-year-old Martin also sprang to his feet, ignoring the bewildered looks of Mama, and running after Christine, he also joined God's House, out of a childhood desire to keep up with his sister.

For Martin, life was a Christmas package. A soft-spoken and easy- going mother, and a devout, warm and easily approachable, dynamic and courageous, hardworking and self-confident father, with a strong sense of justice, steered him forward on his onward journey, robustly supported by a compassionate and affectionate grandmother, Mama, who was suddenly snatched away from their midst when he was only twelve.

Uncritically accepting the Biblical studies up to the age of twelve, he suddenly shocked his Sunday school class by denying the bodily resurrection of Christ, at the age of thirteen.

On 18 May 1941, the air was heavy with the scent of spring flowers. That warm spring day held great promise for twelve-year-old Martin, who stealthily crept out of the house, when the family members thought he was busy studying, and headed towards the Negro business section, with the intention of watching a parade there. Joyously engrossed in the parade, he was brutally jerked out of his enjoyment, when a sad-faced messenger delivered a stunning message to him. Something terrible had happened to Mama. But what could have happened to her? Wasn't she away at Mount Olive Baptist Church speaking in a Women's Day Programme? Maybe the messenger had merely played a cruel prank. Maybe… maybe…!

Many such thoughts raced through his mind, as he hurtled towards his home – a prayer on his lips and apprehension in his heart.

The moment he reached home, his heart sank. The atmosphere was hushed and a lot of morose-looking people stood around. He was told that his beloved Mama, the engrossing raconteur, the compassionate and loving grandmother, who had sobbed uncontrollably when he was beaten and chastised by his disciplinarian father, was no more.

Stunned, the twelve-year-old shattered boy, in a fit of impulsive grief, dashed upstairs and plunged out of the window after his Mama. How could he survive without the warm presence of grandmother Williams? Who would tell him stories? Aghast, people rushed after him to find him still alive, lying on the ground in a painful heap.

Later, in the privacy of his bedroom, he was crushed under the overwhelming emotion of the loss of a dear one. Desolation descended like a flood, not for one day, but for many days. He indulged in self-recrimination, holding himself responsible for the death of his beloved Mama. He had been punished for having sneaked out of the house and having cheated his parents. 'No', his parents told him, 'don't blame what has happened to your grandmother on anything you've done.' But, his mind continued to be plagued by doubts and misgivings for many a day. Racked by guilt, anger and an awful pain, he couldn't sleep at night. The house was filled with Mama's presence, but she was physically absent. The pain of death had slashed its way into his young life. Too young to comprehend the fragility of the thing that the elders called 'life', his world had fallen apart, broken at the seams. Would it ever be set right?

With the loving counseling of his parents, the distraught kid gradually started picking up the threads of his happy life gone awry with the sudden death of his saintly grandmother. But her presence always continued to nestle in a soft corner of his heart.

Although the Kings shifted to a nicer, larger, yellow brick house three blocks away on Boulevard in 1941, when Martin was twelve, it was here in this house, that his initial years were formed and moulded under the patriarchal discipline of Daddy King, the tremendous love and warmth of grandmother Williams – *Mama,* and the motherly care and affection of Alberta – *Mother Dear.*

Martin was later to write that his childhood was very harmonious, with parents *who always lived together very intimately*. 'It is quite easy for me to think of a God of love mainly because I grew up in a family where love was central and lovely relationships were ever present.'[2]

His mother, Alberta, had been a teacher, who had studied in the best available school and college. She was the daughter of Reverend AD Williams who had built Ebenezer Baptist Church into a major institution. Daddy King (Martin Luther King Sr) married Alberta, whom he called Bunch, and later, after his father-in-law's death in the spring of 1931 due to an apoplectic stroke, he became pastor of Ebenezer Baptist Church. Highly ambitious, he got the church renovated, raising its membership from six hundred to many thousands.

Daddy King was not born with a silver spoon in his mouth, but through his never-say-die spirit, sincerity, hard work and dignity, he was able to carve out a comfortable niche for himself in the thriving Atlanta community.

One of ten children, his poor family lived in Stockbridge, Georgia on a plantation outside Atlanta. He left the cotton fields, where his father was a share cropper at the age of eighteen and, carrying his only pair of shoes, he trudged his way to Atlanta – barefooted! The humiliation and subservience of life on the plantation hammered away in his young mind. 'Jim, if you don't keep this nigger boy of yours in his place, I am going to slap him down', his father's boss threatened him when he noticed that he was cheating him of some hard-earned money.

This unlettered youth doggedly slogged his tortuous path through high school and eventually to Morehouse College where, later on, his son would also gain entry. While he was still studying, he started preaching at two churches in Atlanta. It was during this time that he met Alberta, the attractive daughter of Rev. Adam Daniel Williams.

Like his father-in-law, Daddy King also took up cudgels on behalf of those blacks in Atlanta who were vociferous critics of indignities of segregation, refusing to ride segregated buses, fighting for equal pay for black teachers.

'You are as good as anybody' – this was a lesson that Daddy King drilled into his son's mind.

He would often remark thus to Martin, 'Even though the law may force me to ride in the back, my mind is always up front.'

When only a chit of a boy, Martin was taken by his father to a shoe-shop where they sat on a bench in front of the store. They were asked by a clerk to move to the rear if they wanted to buy shoes. Rev King refused point blank, saying that they would either buy shoes sitting where they were, or not at all.

Then head held high, he stomped out of the room, his little son in tow. This was the first time Martin had seen his father so furious, and he realised that his father had not adjusted to the unjust system.

On still another occasion, a policeman stopped them when Daddy King was driving the car, alleging that he had run a stop sign.

'All right, boy ...', the policeman said. An indignant Daddy King retorted, pointing a finger at his son, 'This is a boy. I am a man.'

Later, his father recalled, 'Martin was always a very sensitive child and always above his age in his thinking and his carriage. I would not say he was a peculiar child, but he was a little different in that he always made friends with good books from a small child.'

Honesty, discipline, diligence, courtesy and patience were virtues that the young Martin learnt from his parents.

Martin idolised his father who could be compassionate, affectionate and articulate, but also intimidating at times. His strong sense of justice, fair play and emphasis on truth and non-violence greatly moulded his character. Daddy King could be so brutally frank that the young and the old alike were 'scared to death of him.'

'It is truly better to love than to be loved', Daddy King often mentioned to his family and Martin always tried to follow his father's advice till the day he died.

In his school days, Daddy King had been at the receiving end of many a snide remark. Many of his school chums cruelly called him a *mule*, as he used to work with the mules in a share cropping farm. He later conceded that this had given him a 'mule complex'. One day in utter frustration, he exclaimed, 'I may smell like a mule, but I don't think like a mule.'

The King siblings never felt the sting of economic deprivation although they had been born at a time when the world was on the verge of the disastrous Great Depression. Their father saw to it that they were well provided for – thanks to his art of saving and budgeting, and not of living beyond his means.

When five years of age, the young Martin often questioned his parents about the numerous people standing in breadlines and this scene remained etched in his mind throughout his short life of thirty-nine years, and he often felt guilty about it.

When he was eight years old, his father related an incident

which had a deep impact on him. Bessie Smith, who was a great singer, had an accident, and when an ambulance rushed her to a hospital, she was denied admission, because of her skin colour. She was taken from one hospital to another, but no hospital would take her, as these so-called hospitals catered only to the Whites. Sadly, she died for want of blood.

No doubt they had an idea of the places they could not visit or use, for example, the restrooms or the water fountains which were forbidden to them, but they had a privileged childhood in many ways, sheltered from the assaults of the unjust Jim Crow* laws. But the young Martin was in for a shock when he reached the school age and the mothers of two of his closest white friends forbade their children to play with Martin. Poor Martin was dumbfounded! He had been playing with them all the time before they joined school. On the verge of tears, he rushed home to his mother, who explained to him in soothing tones about slavery, white prejudice and segregation, but also asked him not to cower down under such assaults, 'Don't let this thing make you feel you're not as good as white people.'

---

* Jim Crow laws were state and local laws that enforced racial segregation in the Southern United States. All were enacted in the late 19th and early 20th centuries by white Democratic-dominated state legislatures after the Reconstruction period. The laws were enforced until 1965. The Jim Crow persona was a theater character by Thomas D Rice and an ethnic depiction in accordance with contemporary white ideas of African-Americans and their culture. The character was based on a folk trickster named Jim Crow that was long popular among black slaves. Rice also adapted and popularized a traditional slave song called 'Jump Jim Crow' (1828). The character dressed in rags, battered hat and torn shoes. Rice blackened his face and hands using burnt cork and impersonated a very nimble and irreverently witty African American field hand who sang, "Come listen all you galls and boys, I'm going to sing a little song, my name is Jim Crow..."

Although the young Martin tried his best to feel a sense of 'somebodiness', the unjust system all around him glared at him, reminding him time and again that he was a 'nobody', simply because he was coloured differently. It told him repeatedly: 'You are less than … you are not equal to...'

At the age of eight, the young Martin had a newspaper route, and by the time he reached the age of thirteen, he had risen to the post of Assistant Manager, the youngest assistant manager of a delivery station for the *Atlanta Journal*. Then, in helpless rage, he realised that he could rise no further, because his skin colour came in the way. He realised the colour of one's skin was more important than sincerity and hard work, and only whites could rise to the position of Station Manager.

At the age of fourteen, he had won an oratorical contest sponsored by Negro Elks in Dublin, Georgia. On his way back, suffused with a triumphant glow, he and his teacher, Mrs Bradley, sat in the first available seats in the bus, words from his winning speech, *The Negro and the Constitution*, ringing in his ears: 'The finest Negro is at the mercy of the meanest white man.… So with their right hand, they raise to high places the great who have dark skins, and with their left, they slap us down to keep us in *our places*.' Suddenly, to his shock, the driver of the bus – a white man – ordered him to get up.

Recalling that horrifying incident, Martin said, *'We didn't move quickly enough to suit him, so he began cursing us, calling us black sons of bitches. I intended to stay right in the seat, but Mrs Bradley finally urged me up, saying we had to obey the law. And so, we stood up in the aisle for the ninety miles to Atlanta. That night will never leave my memory. It was the angriest I have ever been in my life.'*[3]

Despite the loving assurances of his mother, that one should always 'feel a sense of somebody-ness' and 'you're as good as anyone else and don't you forget it', the young Martin could not erase those dark memories from his psyche, because the demons of white prejudice would suddenly raise their heads and strike the young, unsuspecting, Martin.

Once, while he stood in front of an Atlanta store, waiting for his mother, he received a stinging slap from a total white stranger. A horrified Martin gaped, as the woman hissed, 'That little nigger stepped on my foot.'

'You know, when I get to be a man, I'm going to hit this thing, and hit it hard, mother; there's no such thing as one people better than another. The Lord made us all equal, and I'm going to see to that,' said Martin to his mother after he had witnessed an argument between his father and a white man.[4]

And he did see to it – with a potent weapon, which involved sit-ins, marches, prayer pilgrimages, and a profound faith in the basic goodness of man. And above all, love – love for the foe, love for the friend, love for the critics, and love even for those with murder on their minds.

'I came to see for the first time that the Christian doctrine of love operating through the Gandhian method of non-violence is one of the most potent weapons available to an oppressed people in their struggle for freedom,' Martin was to say later, but though he used his weapon in Montgomery for the first time, it was provided to him in the loving family environment in which he grew up along with his siblings.

His father's influence was so great on him that after a lot of soul searching, he ultimately decided to follow his father's profession, his admiration for him being the great moving factor.*

This son of great parents, Martin, was bound to touch the heights of greatness. They had carved a path for him, and the young Martin now forged ahead, entering his college years, which further moulded and formed his character.

* At the age of 84, on 11 November 1984, this 'giant of a man', Daddy King, who was compassionate and empathetic, honest and fair, breathed his last at the Crawford W. Long memorial hospital in Atlanta. He had been utterly devastated by the untimely deaths of his two sons in quick succession, Martin in 1968, and AD in 1969, and later on, by the assassination of his loving and devoted wife. For the twenty-three-year old deranged assassin from Ohio, Marcus Wayne Chennault, all Christians were enemies, so he shot Alberta as she played the organ during the Sunday services at the Ebenezer Baptist Church on 30 June 1974. In September 1995, two weeks after suffering a stroke at the state prison in Jackson, the assassin also died; he was 44. At the funeral service of his wife on 3 July 1974, King Sr, a great man, a great husband, a great father, was still able to say, 'I cannot hate any man.'

MOREHOUSE COLLEGE

20 SEPTEMBER 1944 – 8 JUNE 1948

AT THE age of fifteen, this typical teenager, Martin, very fastidious about clothes, who simply loved dancing, meriting the label 'the best jitterbug in town' from his brother, AD, gained admission in Morehouse College, which was his father's alma mater as well as his maternal grandfather's. He began his freshman year on 20 September 1944, eight months after the US Military had introduced blacks into the army.

Founded in 1867 and located on a 66-acre campus on 830 West-view Drive, SW Atlanta, and also known as the Negro Harvard, the mission of this private, liberal arts, college for men was to develop men with disciplined minds, who would lead lives of leadership and service, and be committed to social justice.

One of the corollaries of black participation in World War II was the drastic decrease in the number of enrollments in historically black colleges, Morehouse College being one of them. Faced with this crisis, Benjamin E Mays, the president of Morehouse flung open its exalted gates to those high school juniors who showed marks of diligence. Martin applied to this early admission programme and was selected.

He spent five years of his teenage life in this all-black college amid intellectual giants who were greatly instrumental in honing and shaping his ideology.

In the first two years of his college life, he was in a dilemma – about which career should he embark on, Law or Medicine? Eventually, he opted for Sociology. Despite the influence of his parents, he was not very keen on joining the ministry, although he could imagine himself playing an important role in breaking the legal barriers to Negro rights. Deeply interested in social ills and political matters, he would often shoot off letters to the newspaper editors regarding rampant racial injustice.

It was here that he was initiated into the philosophy of Henry David Thoreau, making his first contact with the 'theory of non-violent resistance'. He was so fascinated by the essay on *Civil Disobedience* that he read it many a time. Thoreau's teachings came alive in the civil rights movement 'whether expressed in a sit-in at lunch counters, a freedom ride into Mississippi, a peaceful protest in Albany, Georgia, a bus boycott in Montgomery Alabama; these are the outgrowths of Thoreau's insistence that evil must be resisted and that no moral man can patiently adjust to injustice.'[1]

It was here in the college that many of his doubts were cleared, and many were formed. He wondered how the 'facts of science could be squared with religion'; he was embarrassed by the 'emotionalism' of the Negro religion and 'the shouting and stamping' that it involved. He also wondered whether religion 'could serve as a vehicle to modern thinking, whether religion could be intellectually respectable as well as emotionally satisfying.'[2]

It was here amid the ivy-coloured buildings, that he found the academic freedom to openly discuss the evils of segregation and talk about the role of leadership in liberating the Negro.

King Collection, Morehouse College

Despite his instinctive knowledge that church was the black man's refuge from the stings of discrimination, despite the heritage of his father and maternal grandfather, despite an intuitive feeling that his father wanted him to join the ministry, he felt he was not cut out for the job of a pastor, and had already begun to 'reject the fire and brimstone tradition of his father and grandfather as un-intellectual and as irrelevant to the daily life of the oppressed Southern black'.[3]

He was strongly convinced that he could help in the liberation of his people by joining some other profession, but later events made him reconsider his decision not to join the ministry.

During his summer vacation, he travelled along with his friends from Morehouse to Connecticut to pick tobacco, and to widen his horizons. This visit was a cultural shock for them. To their pleasant surprise, they realised that no Jim Crow Laws glared at them at that place. They were free to enter restaurants, movie theatres and other public places. However, some subtle forms of racism, which was prevalent there also, failed to register on their young minds.

But, alas! The collegian King had to swallow another 'bitter pill' when he was forced to sit behind a curtain in the dining car, while returning home from Morehouse college. He felt 'as if a curtain had dropped on my selfhood'.

At Morehouse, he came in contact with some great minds and their views had a direct bearing upon his thinking pattern.

Dr Benjamin Elijah Mays, the distinguished president of Morehouse, and also a friend of Daddy King, recognised the spark in Martin, and this illustrious preacher soon became his 'spiritual mentor', greatly impacting his ultimate decision to follow into the footsteps of his father and grandfather.

Remembered for his outstanding leadership and service as a teacher, preacher, author and an activist in the civil rights movement, Dr Mays, born on 1 August 1894, became the sixth president of Morehouse College in 1940, launching a twenty-seven-year tenure during which it catapulted into international prominence.

Enormously impressed by the philosophy of this tall and erudite man, and his teachings of stewardship, responsibility and liberation, Martin realised that the church could be an effective institution for social protests. In Mays, Martin found a 'rational man whose sermons were both spiritually and intellectually stimulating, a moral man who was socially involved'.[4]

Martin was so impressed by Mays' Tuesday morning chapel talks, that he would often follow his professor into his office for further clarification. His talks were liberally sprinkled with words like, 'brotherhood of man', 'the fatherhood of God', 'ethical laws' and this language crept into Martin's vocabulary and into his prolific writings.

Mays drilled into his students the imperative need to rebel against injustice and unfairness. He said, 'The only way they could be free in a rigidly segregated society was by consistent refusal ever to accept subservience and segregation in their own minds.'[5]

Mays also said, 'It will not be sufficient for Morehouse College, or for any college, for that matter, to produce clever graduates, men fluent in speech and able to argue their way through, but rather honest men, men who can be trusted in public and private – who are sensitive to the wrongs, the sufferings and the injustices of society and who are willing to accept responsibility for correcting the ills.'

Mays' ideology would resonate through Martin's speeches years later. His views on social democracy, social gospel, the positive role of the state and the church would be reflected in his writings, such as the *Letter from Birmingham Jail*: 'If today's church does not recapture the sacrificial spirit of the early church, it will lose its authenticity, forfeit the loyalty of millions, and be dismissed as an irrelevant social club with no meaning for the twentieth century.'

Besides Mays, other professor-preachers also pushed and prodded Martin's subconscious urge to become a preacher. Their 'social gospel' appealed to the young Martin, and he found it socially relevant and intellectually stimulating. Gone was his dithering and confusion. Now, it dawned on him that: 'The ministry could be intellectually meaningful as well as emotionally inspiring … that the pulpit was the most direct route to his people. The tradition of the Southern Baptist preacher-orator was a strong one. Nowhere else did a man have a captive audience so willing as to follow where he might lead.'[6]

Gladstone Lewis Chandler, affectionately known as GLC by his students, was their professor of English. Martin described him as 'one of the most articulate, knowledgeable and brilliant professors' at Morehouse college, who excelled at playing word games with his students. He coerced them into enriching their vocabulary, and prodded them into honing their style.

On the very first day of English composition, he would declare, 'We are going to establish a "GLC word-bank". You deposit some new words in each class session, invest them in congenial conversation and withdraw rich dividends.'

Martin, who was very fond of this English professor, did indeed draw 'rich dividends' from the GLC word-bank, investing new and powerful words in his oratory, and GLC, as Martin later admitted in his memoirs, was a great influence on him.

'Chandler was a demanding task master for his students. But he seemingly had the gift for leading the young men under his charge to a more articulate way of writing and speaking.'[7]

During his sojourn in Connecticut in the summer vacation,

Martin was asked to lead the devotions for the students in the tobacco farm. That was another turning point in his life. He rediscovered himself, started reading the scriptures, and mesmerised the students with his oratorical skills, having inherited them and a sense of language from two generations – his father and maternal grandfather.

In an effort to understand the rampant cruelty, injustice and segregation, he turned to books. With a bibliophile's zeal, he tried to read anything that he could, about the civil war, slavery and about the history of the blacks. He was organising and preparing himself for the fight ahead.

Walter Chivers

'Money is not only the root of evil; it is also the root of this particular evil – racism', this dictum of his Sociology professor, Walter Chivers, from whom Martin took seven courses, would permeate his entire philosophy in his later life. As Martin Luther King Jr turned from Civil Rights to Human Rights in 1967-68, the lessons he learnt at Morehouse College were always there at the back of his mind – that cultural deficiencies or family pathologies were not always responsible for poverty, but unequal wealth was. His vision of economic freedom had taken shape in classrooms of Morehouse College.

'King's later works included not only the sweeping themes of Mays' vision of social democracy but also the concrete realism of sociologist Walter Chivers.'[8]

'It was not the student non-violent coordinating committee that first introduced King to the practical wisdom of including dispossessed youth in the Civil Rights movement. The political realism of Walter Chivers entered King's thought long before Black Power and SNCC* even existed.'[9]

'*Of course, I was religious. I grew up in the Church. My father is a preacher, my grandfather was a preacher, my great grandfather was a preacher, my only brother is a preacher, my daddy's brother is a preacher, so I didn't have much choice.*' Martin uttered these words later when, after a lot of intellectual churning in Morehouse College, he decided to follow his father's and grandfather's footsteps and joined the ministry.[10]

The cobwebs had finally cleared from his mind and much to his father's elation, he wrote to his mother, 'You know, Daddy won't believe me, but I'm going to preach.'

On hearing this, Daddy King wondered whether Martin was serious. When confronted by his father, with a confident elation, Martin remarked, 'Yes sir, I'm going to preach.'

On being told by his father, that he would not be able to earn any money by preaching but, if he became a lawyer, he could earn a lot, a determined Martin rejoined that he would preach for nothing, and he would never worry about money, and he was true to his word.

In his 1950 essay, *An Autobiography of Religious Development*, Martin wrote that he had been greatly influenced by his father in his choice of profession, '*I guess the influence of my father also had a great deal to do with my going in the ministry. This is not to say that he even spoke to me in terms of being a minister, but that my admiration for him was the great moving factor; he set forth a noble example that I didn't mind following.*'

* The Student Nonviolent Coordinating Committee

In one of the small chapels of the church, Daddy King arranged a trial sermon for him and some of those who heard that sermon were surprised by the maturity of the boy.

So even before he finished college, he was ordained and given full credentials. Each summer he came back to work with his father.

In 1947, at the age of eighteen and still a junior in college, he was made the assistant pastor of Ebenezer Baptist Church. Apart from working as assistant pastor, Martin also tried his hand at an assortment of jobs. While working at Railway Express and the Southern Spring Bed Mattress Company, he learnt another bitter truth: that there was no pay parity as far as blacks were concerned. Blacks were paid less than whites for equal work.

He was, however, under no financial compulsion to endure the humiliation of his white bosses. So when a derogatory word 'nigger' was hurled at him by a foreman, he decided to quit his job.

In his book, *Stride toward Freedom*, he explained that he had been greatly moved by Thoreau's essay on *the duty of civil disobedience* and fascinated by Thoreau's idea of refusing to cooperate with an evil system.[11] Like Thoreau, Martin was being true to his conscience, by refusing to be part of a system which was an assault on his personal dignity, or maybe the words that his mother had drilled into him on an earlier occasion '*Don't let this thing make you feel you're not as good as white people*', or his father's words, '*you are as good as anybody*' that prodded him into quitting this job.

AT CROZER SEMINARY

14 SEPT 1948 – 8 MAY 1951

ARMED WITH formidable knowledge gained from intellectual giants, Martin graduated from Morehouse College at the age of nineteen and went to study Divinity at Crozer Theological Seminary in Chester Pennsylvania, on a scholarship. One of a half dozen black students amongst a total of 100 students, he became the first black student ever to be elected as the president of the student body.

Here at the seminary, he became a serious bibliophile, reading any book that caught his fancy. In a letter, dated October 1948, he wrote to his mother, '*I never go anywhere much, but in these books ... I am too busy studying.*'

He also tried desperately to 'overcome' what he felt was the Negro stereotype, making lasting friendships, even among some of the white students.

'I was well aware of the typical white stereotype of the Negro, that he is always late, that he's loud and always laughing, that he's dirty and messy, and for a while, I was terribly conscious of trying to avoid identification with it. If I were a minute late to class, I was almost morbidly conscious of it and sure that everyone else noticed it. Rather than being thought of as always laughing, I'm afraid I was grimly serious for a time. I had a tendency to overdress, to keep my room spotless, my shoes perfectly shined, and my clothes immaculately pressed.'[1]

It was here that a serious intellectual churning started in his mind. Greatly stimulated by the social and ethical theories of Plato, Aristotle, Rousseau, Hobbes, Bentham, Mill and Locke, he also read Walter Rauschenbusch's *Christianity and the Social Crisis*. Ever since reading Rauschenbusch, he was strongly convinced, that any religion that professes concern for the souls of men and is not equally concerned about the slums that damn them, the economic conditions that strangle them, and the social conditions that cripple them, is a spiritually moribund religion only waiting for the day to be buried.[2]

During his seminary days, he reached the conclusion that a preaching minister should not only be a spellbinding orator, but he should also have spiritual power. He should not leave the people 'lost in the fog of theological abstraction', but his preaching should grow out of the experiences of people.

As an aspirant for the ministry, it was his mission to transform the souls of individuals so that their societies may also transform and to transform the societies so that the individual souls would be transformed. With that aim in mind, he wanted to improve the condition of slums, address unemployment and economic insecurity.

During the Christmas holidays of 1949, he delved deep into *Das Kapital* and the *Communist Manifesto,* and reached the conclusion that, although communism is 'basically evil', being based on 'false assumptions and evil methods', it cannot be denied that it grew in revolt against the hardships of the underprivileged, it was concerned about social justice, and emphasised a classless society.

Yet, he believed that, in practice, it created 'new classes and a new lexicon of injustice'. He outrightly rejected its materialistic interpretation of history, its ethical relativism, its political totalitarianism, its depreciation of individual freedom.

However, on the basis of his reading of Marx, he became acutely conscious of the gulf between superfluous wealth and abject poverty and was firmly convinced of the need of a better distribution of wealth. He concluded: 'Truth is found neither in Marxism nor in traditional capitalism.... Historically, capitalism failed to see the truth in collective enterprise and Marxism failed to see the truth in individual enterprise.... The Kingdom of God is neither the thesis of individual enterprise nor the antithesis of collective enterprise, but a synthesis which reconciles the truth of both'.

It was while reading parts of Nietzsche's *The Genealogy of Morals* and the whole of *The Will to Power* that a sort of scepticism regarding the power of love, in solving social problems crept into his mindset. He started believing that only through an armed revolt could the problem of segregation be solved. Nietzsche's idea of the superman who would surpass man, as man had surpassed the ape, somehow appealed to his young mind, his equating piety and humility with weakness seemed to make sense to him. But then came a turning point in his life.

One Sunday afternoon, he travelled to Philadelphia to hear a sermon by Mordecai Johnson, President of Howard University. Fresh from a trip to India, Johnson spoke of the life and teachings of **Mahatma Gandhi.** So 'profound and electrifying' was his message that he immediately went and bought half dozen books on Gandhi's life and works.

Deeply fascinated by his campaigns of non-violent resistance, the Salt March, his fasts, *satyagraha*, Martin's scepticism regarding the power of love as an instrument of social and collective transformation diminished. Now for the first time, he realised the potency of the weapon of love in the sphere of social reform. Earlier, he had started believing that the ethics of Jesus could be useful only in individual relations, but now he realised 'how utterly mistaken' he was.

In his words, '*The intellectual and moral satisfaction that I failed to gain from the utilitarianism of Bentham and Mill, the revolutionary method of Marx and Lenin, the social contract theory of Hobbes, the 'back to nature' optimism of Rousseau, the superman philosophy of Nietzsche, I found in the nonviolent resistance philosophy of Gandhi.*'

In his senior year in theological seminary, he was knocked out of his 'dogmatic slumber' when he read various theological theories. Earlier, he had accepted the liberal interpretation of Christianity with unquestioning ease, but now he started to question the liberal doctrine of man. Certain experiences he had in the South, with its evil racial problem, made him doubt the intrinsic goodness of man. He came to feel that '*liberalism had been all too sentimental concerning human nature and that it leaned toward a false idealism.*' But at the same time, he realised that the noble possibilities of human nature could not be downplayed. There was one phase of liberalism, which he always cherished, and that was its devotion to the search for the Truth.

During his last year in theological school, he started to read the works of Reinhold Niebuhr. His writings made him recognise the '*illusions of a superficial optimism concerning human nature and the dangers of a false idealism.*' While still believing in man's potential for goodness, Niebuhr made him realise his potential for evil as well. This American theologian had abandoned the doctrine of pacifism in favour of 'Christian realism.'

In the beautiful environs of the seminary campus, he also tried to strengthen his spiritual life through communion with Nature. In bounteous nature – the stars, the sun, the moon, the birds, the leaves, and the rippling waves – he found the reflection of God.

Impact of Walter Rauschenbusch

In his book, *Stride toward Freedom,* Martin acknowledged 'the indelible imprint' that Rauschenbusch's work *Christianity and the Social Crisis* left on his thinking.

During his theological training at Rochester Theological Seminary, Rauschenbusch had started believing that the primary responsibility of the Church is to lead individuals to seek their personal salvation. But, it was later, as pastor of the second German Baptist Church of New York, that he developed a passion for social reform, when he witnessed the desperation and ugliness of the lives of his parishioners. His parish was situated near Hell's Kitchen, one of New York's worst slums.

Explaining his passion, he maintained that, due to his personal contact with poverty, he was witness to many heart-wrenching scenes – the sight of strong bodied men begging, small children's deaths and funerals, men toiling diligently and receiving a pittance in return, all smote at his heart.

Rauschenbusch's impact on Martin was evident in his crusades. About the Christian Church, Rauschenbusch said that it 'should be swiftest to awaken to every undeserved suffering, bravest to speak against every wrong, and strongest to rally the moral forces of the community against everything that threatens the better life among men'.

Time and again, Martin reminded his ministers of their social mission, exhorting them to try to change the environmental conditions of millions who go to bed hungry.

The monster of racial prejudice stalked him even in Crozer. Once, when he and his friends had gone to a restaurant, the restaurant owner refused to serve them, even threatening them physically. Although Martin and his friends tried to take this case to the court, the suit was dropped when no witness testified.

In another incident, a North Carolinian white student, with extremely racist views, one day came banging at his door; someone had messed up his room and he thought it was Martin. Hurling abuses at him, he even drew out a gun. Undeterred, Martin refused to be cowed down. The students intervened and made him down his gun. The matter was brought before the student government but Martin refused to press charges. The chastened North Carolinian conceded that he was wrong and publicly apologised. The two later became good friends. The young Martin, in typical Gandhian style, had converted an enemy into a friend.

This incident catapulted Martin into immediate popularity, his elegant charm, disarming smile and sharp intellect floored many a girl, and he became the most sought-after student at Crozer, graduating with a Bachelor of Divinity in 1951, having secured straight As. This class valedictorian went on to win the Pearl Plafker Award for the most outstanding student. A delighted Daddy King gave him a car in honour of his graduation and in the fall, he loaded this green Chevrolet with his possessions and headed towards Boston, having won a $1,300 scholarship to the graduate school of his choice.

KING AT BOSTON UNIVERSITY

13 SEPTEMBER 1951 – 5 JUNE 1955

IN APRIL 1965, when Martin went to Boston to lead a march protesting Negro discontent with housing, jobs and schools, he told the Massachusetts' Republican Governor, John A Volpe, that having lived in Boston for four years, he felt Boston was one of the cities that he considered part of his home. He had entered this home on 13 September 1951, as a student of Boston University's School of Theology, receiving his doctorate in Systematic Theology on 5 June 1955. His dissertation was titled, '*A Comparison of God in the thinking of Paul Tillich and Henry Wieman.*'

The university was characterised by Raymond Bean, one of Martin's favourite professors at Crozer, as 'a hospitable environment for African American students', and he had recommended that Martin study Personalism with Edgar Sheffield Brightman at Boston. Professor Bean himself was a graduate of Boston University.

Personalism emerged as a philosophic movement in the early 1900s. Having a number of affinities with Christianity, its focus was on the sanctity of persons and a personal God.

Martin translated Personalism into action, believing that person is the supreme philosophical principle without which no other principle can be understood, that the Universe is a society of interacting and intercommunicating selves and persons with God at the center.

'In his search for a place to stand, King encountered Nietzsche, Marx and Gandhi, among others. It was the movement known as Personalism that made the most lasting impression upon King's mind. Personalism was to be linked with Gandhi's non-violent ethic as a means to oppose the evils of racist oppression.'[1]

Going beyond his teachers in applying Personalism, Martin certainly mined the school of Personalism for all its worth. He road-tested this point of view in his freedom activities. Furthermore, his Personalism developed and matured in a hostile environment and against all odds.[2]

Every person, be it a scavenger, a rag-picker or a sweeper is heir to a legacy of dignity and worth. There is no graded scale of essential worth. The indelible stamp of the creator has been etched in every personality; hence, none can be exploited, oppressed, beaten or butchered.

Vibrant and relevant, '*the meaning of King's Personalism was worked out in the struggle for dignity and justice, rather than in the relative comfort of the classroom or a cozy study*'.[3]

In his application to Boston University in 1950, Martin had stated, that his 'thinking in philosophical areas has been greatly influenced by some of the faculty members there, particularly Dr Brightman' (King papers 1: 390).

Five years after the death of Dr Brightman, Martin wrote that his mentor from Boston University's School of Theology had given him the '*metaphysical and philosophical grounding for the idea of a personal God*' (King papers 4:480).

While he was at Crozer, Martin had become aware of Brightman's ideas. He read Brightman's *A philosophy of Religion* (1940) and commented: '*How I long now for that religious experience which Dr Brightman so cogently speaks of throughout his book. It seems to be an experience, the lack of which makes life dull and meaningless*' (King papers 1: 415-416).

It was this philosophy of Personalism that was uppermost on his mind when he spoke of improving the condition of the sanitation workers, when he spoke of calling halt to the Vietnam War, when he tried to solve the problem of racism, exploitation and militarism.

This professionally trained philosopher, civil rights leader, Nobel laureate, and an apostle of non-violence owes a colossal debt to the philosophers who shaped his convictions and beliefs, first, as an undergraduate at Morehouse College, later at Crozer Seminary, and eventually at Boston University. Later, he was to have a '*world-wide impact on large numbers of ordinary citizens and in the halls of government*'.[4]

Martin had gone to Boston in clear pursuit of a greater knowledge of Personalism. Later, this philosophy became the basis of his quest for social justice. In the stimulating environs of Boston University, he had the opportunity to talk to many exponents of non-violence; thus, strengthening his philosophy of non-violence.

Dean Walter Muelder and Professor Allan Knight Chalmers had an abiding influence on him. Both were passionate about social justice, and this passion, Martin believed, did not stem from 'a superficial optimism concerning human nature, but from a deep faith in the possibilities of human beings when they allowed themselves to become co-workers with God'.[5]

He studied philosophy and theology under Edgar S Brightman and L Harold Dewolff, and the philosophy of Personalism – 'the theory that the clue to the meaning of ultimate reality is found in personality', was eventually to become the cornerstone of his beliefs. From this stemmed his strong conviction in the dignity and worth of the human personality.

After just about 16 months of Martin's joining Boston University, Edgar S Brightman died, on 25 February 1953. Before his death, Martin had started delving into the intricacies of Hegelian philosophy under his able guidance. He read Hegel's magnum opus *Phenomenology of Mind* and also his

Philosophy of History and *Philosophy of Right.*

Although he did not agree with Hegel's absolute idealism, his contention that truth is whole, led him to a philosophical method of rational coherence. His entire perspective on reality was shaped by Hegelian logic.

In Boston, he shared an apartment with Philip Lenud, a friend from Morehouse College, who was studying divinity at Tufts University. They founded the Philosophical Club, which was meant to be an all-male, all-black informal forum for discussion on philosophical issues. Soon this group had a wider membership, no longer remaining all-black, or all-male.

In January 1952, Martin met a young charming woman from Alabama, Coretta Scott, who, he felt had all the qualities he was looking for in his wife. A mutual admiration grew between the two. Coretta later confessed, '*He was different from the stereotype I had envisioned. He was good – such a very good man.*'

She started accompanying him to the meetings of the Philosophical Club, talking passionately about ideas of all kinds. Martin soon learned that Coretta, like him, severely opposed racism and segregation. To others, he appeared serious and intense but with Coretta, he was full of fun and humour.

'I'll come over and pick you up. I have a green Chevy that usually takes ten minutes to make the trip from BU, but tomorrow, I'll do it in seven', twenty-three year old Martin gushed over the phone to Coretta Scott whose 'gentle manners and air of repose', the strength of quiet determination, her talent for music, her compassion and sense of fair play had greatly enthralled him.

They married on 18 June 1953 on the sprawling lawns of the Scott's house in Marion, Alabama, and then returned to Boston to begin their married life together.

In Boston, Martin was expected to complete the residency requirement for his PhD and Coretta wished to continue her music education. In their four-room apartment, both shared the household chores. Every Friday evening, they went to the Philosophical Club. Martin often preached at nearby churches. She was able to give him a '*well-ordered home where Christian love is a reality*' and he warmly conceded later, '*If I had not had a wife with the fortitude, strength and calmness of Coretta, I could not have withstood the ordeals and tensions surrounding the movement.*'[6]

They had four children: Yolanda 'Yoki' Denise King, born on 17 November 1955, in Montgomery.[7]

Martin Luther III was born on 23 October 1957, in Montgomery, Alabama.

Dexter Scott King, their third child was born on 30 January 1961, in Atlanta, Georgia.

Bernice Albertine King was born on 28 March 1963, in Atlanta, Georgia.

In early 1954, Martin started looking for a position that would give him an opportunity to work for the black people. Offers poured in from the South and also from the North, but Coretta was not very keen on a job in the South, being aware of the intense hatred the blacks faced in Alabama, but Martin was convinced that the South needed him.

So he accepted an offer to give a trial sermon at the Dexter Avenue Baptist Church in Montgomery, Alabama. His sermon was titled, '*The Three Dimensions of a Complete Life.*' He was unanimously chosen as pastor of this upper-middle-class black Church on a salary of forty-two hundred dollars, which was the highest salary ever paid to any black minister in Montgomery.

Accepting this offer, he gave his first sermon as the pastor of the Dexter Avenue Baptist Church in May 1954. Soon the congregation started appreciating his sincere and compassionate oratorical style.

It was also in May 1954 that the United States Supreme Court ordered the desegregation of all schools in the revolutionary *Brown vs Board of Education* decision, which precipitated a growing unrest in Montgomery. 'Martin Luther King Jr had no plan and only the dimmest vision of his future when he took up his post in this "Cradle of the Confederacy."'[8]

This small church had a congregation of only three hundred as compared to four thousand at his father's church in Atlanta. But Martin's congregation comprised the influential black citizens – professionals, businessmen, intellectuals and these people would soon see in him a leader, a symbol of hope, an eloquent man who could very powerfully articulate their innermost feelings.

Martin had no idea that Montgomery would catapult him into international prominence, and he would be instrumental in infusing a new self-respect in the Southern Negro, giving birth to a 'New Negro' unshackled from the emasculating manacles of the past.

In June 1955, Martin was awarded his PhD from Boston University, and in the same month, the United States Supreme Court reaffirmed its desegregation decision of 1954, adding that this desegregation should be implemented 'with all deliberate speed'. But this created only a ripple in Montgomery, no tangible step was taken to implement it.

At this time, there was rampant passivity in the blacks of Montgomery. Although the whites proudly proclaimed the existence of peaceful racial relations, this peace was a deceptive peace, a result of unreasoning submission on the part of the blacks.

There was a woeful lack of cohesive leadership in Montgomery, although certain groups like *The Citizens Committee, Progressive Democrats, Women's Political Council,* valiantly tried to fight segregation. Though tired of the humiliation, they were willing to endure it because of their homes and hearths being in Montgomery.

But then things changed on 1 December 1955, when Rosa Parks, a respected seamstress of Montgomery's black community, refused to give her seat to a white man in a segregated bus.

MONTGOMERY BUS BOYCOTT

5 DECEMBER 1955 – 20 DECEMBER 1956

THIS WAS the first large-scale demonstration against racial segregation in the USA, and a critical moment in the history of American civil rights. On 1 December 1955, Rosa Parks, also known as Rosa Louise McCauley, an African-American seamstress, refused to vacate her seat on a bus for a white passenger in Montgomery, Alabama, which was violative of the city's racial segregation ordinances. Besides her, there were two others who complied. However, Rosa's refusal triggered the movement for racial equality and the first step in the path of the realisation of the American Dream.

In the words of Martin, Rosa Parks was 'anchored to that seat by the accumulated indignities of days gone by and the boundless aspirations of generations yet unborn.' Her refusal to get up, heralded the Montgomery bus boycott, inaugurating the civil rights era, catapulting Martin Luther King Jr into the international scene, and drawing the curtains on segregation in the South.

This iconic woman, who grew up without a father, recalls in her autobiography, *Rosa Parks: My Story*, the nights she spent next to her grandfather's gun, ears pricked for the Klan*, and she had, with one small act of protest, changed the course of American history in a big way.

Her arrest on 1 December 1955, following her refusal to vacate the seat reserved for white passengers, unleashed a storm of protest, which was followed by the unanimous decision of boycotting these segregated buses. According to the local laws, the black passengers were expected to sit at the back of the bus while whites sat in front. If the white section became full, it was mandatory for the blacks to give up their seats for white passengers in the back section of the bus.

Rosa Parks with Martin Luther King Jr in the background

When Parks refused to move from her seat, she was taken to jail; and later bailed out.

Twenty-six-year-old King Jr, then pastor of Montgomery's Dexter Avenue Baptist Church, was elected president of the newly formed *Montgomery Improvement Association*, and he spearheaded the boycott, which was initially a one-day protest on five

* The Ku Klux Klan is an American white supremacist hate group that has existed since the 1860s.

December, but went on to last for 381 days. Slowly, it gathered momentum, and approximately 40,000 blacks participated in the boycott.

A lot of careful planning and coordination went into the execution of the boycott, working with a 'grim and bold determination to gain justice in the buses in the city'.

During this period, they had to face many setbacks – there were slur campaigns, bombings and threats, but King Jr exhorted his brethren to adhere strictly to the philosophy of non-violence. '*Let us keep moving,*' he said, '*with the faith that what we are doing is right and with the even greater faith that God is with us in the struggle.*' They set up an effective car pool, which had 300 private cars cruising the streets. There were many stories of valour and single-minded determination as even arthritic octogenarians brusquely turned down offers of a lift in the cars provided by the pool service. With glowing faces and straight backs, they walked on, robustly maintaining that they were not walking for themselves, but for their grandkids. Cooks and maids walked endless miles for a year to make a dent in the ugly wall of segregation.

On 5 June 1956, a Montgomery federal court ruled that the 14th Amendment of the US Constitution, adopted in 1868, guaranteeing all citizens – regardless of race – equal rights and equal protection under state and federal laws, would be violated, if racial segregation was followed in buses. This was followed by the Supreme Court upholding the lower court's decision on 20 December 1956. Consequently, on 21 December 1956, blacks and whites in Montgomery rode for the first time on previously segregated buses.

The bus boycott brought about a positive change in the collective black psyche in Montgomery. Racial shame diminished, and a new sense of dignity was injected in them and as, King Jr later maintained, 'The once dormant and quiescent Negro community was now fully awake.'

However, this awakening of a 'quiescent conscience' was not without violent repercussions.

The aftermath

How could the race supremacists tolerate this assault on the centennial status quo? Consequently, there were sniper attacks on buses, and segregated bus stops continued to be maintained in Montgomery. The Ku Klux Klan ('KKK') resorted to bomb attacks; four black churches were bombed and on 30 January 1957 seven KKK bombers were arrested.

In February 1957, King Jr was featured on the cover of *Time*: 'King reached beyond law books and writs, beyond violence and threats to win his people – and challenge all people with a spiritual force that aspired even to ending prejudice in man's mind.... He struck where an attack was least expected, and where it hurt most: at the Southern Christian Conscience.' A hitherto unknown face was catapulted to the center of the civil rights movement.

Southern Christian Leadership Conference (SCLC)

Responding to King's call for a meeting, more than sixty black ministers committed to Southern Civil Rights Movement met on 10 and 11 January 1957 and formed the *Southern Christian Leadership Conference.*

It met formally for the first time in New Orleans on 14 February 1957; King Jr was unanimously elected the first president of this new organisation, which he served till his death.

Dr Joseph E Lowery, the third president of the SCLC, called it the '*cutting edge, the moral voice, the prophetic outcry, the independent force in the struggle ... the vehicle ... the chair that Martin rode and drove through the turbulence of the late fifties and sixties.*'

Many years later, King Jr articulated five fundamental goals of the SCLC: 'First, to stimulate non-violent direct mass action to expose and remove the barriers of segregation and discrimination; second, to disseminate the creative philosophy and techniques of non-violence through local and area workshops; third, to secure the right and unhampered use of the ballot for every citizen; fourth, to achieve full citizenship rights, and the total integration of the Negro into American life and fifth, to reduce the cultural lag through our citizenship training program.'

The SCLC appealed to President Dwight Eisenhower and the Vice President Richard Nixon, in their preliminary meeting, to call a White House conference on Civil Rights, warning them that if they did not take remedial steps, SCLC would be forced to initiate a mighty Prayer Pilgrimage to Washington.

An AP photo of Eisenhower and Nixon, taken about 60 years ago.

Prayer pilgrimage to Washington: Give us the Ballot

The 'moment is unpropitious'; they were politely informed by the White House, so now the Prayer Pilgrimage appeared inevitable.

On 17 May 1957, three years after the *Brown vs Board Of Education* decision, King Jr participated in the pilgrimage, delivering his first major national address, calling for black voting rights, which established him as the foremost black leader of his era.

On this momentous day, 37,000 marchers stood before the Lincoln Memorial having come from all parts of the country. Among the marchers were celebrities like, Harry Belafonte, Sammy Davis Jr, Jackie Robinson, Sidney Poitier, Mahalia Jackson, and also nearly three thousand white people.

As the programme got under way, there were inspiring speeches by Mordecai Johnson, Philip Randolph, Roy Wilkins, Adam Powell, and a song from the legendary singer, Mahalia Jackson.

Mahalia Jackson, the famous singer.

It was at 3 pm when King Jr was introduced by Randolph. Thunderous applause followed pin drop silence, as King Jr's baritone rang out – clear and passionate. Using the antiphony and familiar cadence of the Baptist Church, King Jr spoke thus:

'Give us the ballot – and we will no longer plead to the federal government for the passage of an anti-lynching law. Give us the ballot – and we will transform the salient misdeeds of blood-thirsty mobs into the abiding good deeds of orderly citizens. Give us the ballot – and we will fill our legislative halls with men of good will! Give us the ballot – and we will get the people judges who love mercy. Give us the ballot – and we will quietly, lawfully implement the May 17, 1954, decision of the Supreme Court.'

He criticised the Eisenhower government as, 'too silent and apathetic', and assailed the Congress as, 'too stagnant and hypocritical', lashed out at the 'blatant hypocrisy of the right wing', at '*the high blood pressure of words and an anemia of deeds.*' Catching the beat, the audience chorused, *Give us the Ballot,* punctuating King Jr's mesmerising words with 'amens', 'yeahs' and 'hallelujahs'.

A couple of days after the Prayer Pilgrimage, when he preached at Philadelphia's Zion Baptist Church, the church was choc-a-bloc, and there were many more people outside, very keen to catch a glimpse of this charismatic leader who had suddenly gained popularity on the basis of his fiery oratorical skills.

Later, New York's *Amsterdam News* wrote: 'King Jr emerged from the prayer pilgrimage to Washington as the number one leader of sixteen million Negroes in the United States.'

In the same month, he was awarded the NAACP's Spingarn Medal* for his contribution to race relations, the youngest person to get it.

Other important events followed, some at the political front, some at the domestic front.

Conferences with President Eisenhower & Nixon

In June 1957, King Jr and Ralph Abernathy had a two-hour conference with Vice President Nixon, where they pressed the demands made earlier by SCLC. However, there was only one tangible result of this meeting – another conference on 23 June 1958, but this time with President Eisenhower – attended by King Jr, Randolph, Ray Wilkins and Lester B Granger.

Philip Randolph presented a nine-point programme on

---

* National Association for the Advancement of Colored People - NAACP

behalf of the group, which, however, failed to have any apparent impact on the Eisenhower administration.

In September 1957, King Jr became the proud father of his first son and namesake, Martin Luther King III.

During this time, he was busy completing the manuscript of his book, *Stride toward Freedom*, which was finally delivered to the publisher in February 1958. He was also assisting Lawrence Reddick in preparing a biography of himself. By now, his commitment to pacifism and non-violence was total. He gave many forceful speeches during this time. In one of his most forceful speeches in Florida, he said: 'To Negro Americans, it is ironic to be governed, to be taxed, to be given orders, but to have no representation in a nation that would defend the right to vote abroad.... Let us make our intentions crystal clear. We must and we will be free. We want freedom now.... We do not want freedom fed to us in teaspoons over another 150 years.... We Southerners, Negro and White, must no longer permit our heritage to be dishonored before the world....'[1]

The third of September 1958, was another dark day in King's life when the bitter stings of racial prejudice again attacked him viciously.

The Kings had gone to Montgomery's Recorder Court along with the Abernathys, where Ralph Abernathy was to testify against a man who had assaulted him, when King was seized by two guards, thrust down the Court House steps, and hauled inside the police station. They pushed him roughly into a cell, snapping and growling at him.

On 5 September, he was found guilty of refusing to obey an officer and fined 10 dollars plus costs – the same amount that had been levied against Rosa Parks. He decided to go to jail, instead of paying the fine, but even before he could be transported to jail, he was released! Clyde C Sellers, the Montgomery Police Commissioner had paid the fine, not due to any pang of remorse but as he said in a statement that he had '*elected to spare the taxpayers of Montgomery the expense of feeding and housing (King) during the next fourteen years.... He couldn't possibly have permitted King to use the jail for "his own selfish purposes", as a "publicity stunt"*'.

Meanwhile, Ralph Abernathy along with some 200 black citizens had started an impromptu protest march from the courthouse to Dexter Avenue Baptist Church. While they were engaged in a meeting, King suddenly arrived and took over.

'*We must go out of this meeting with the determination to take a firm and courageous stand against police brutality. We must no longer be afraid to go to jail,*' he vowed, and pledged never again to pay a fine for any charge arising from '*our fight for freedom*'.

INDIA CONNECT

RANGANATH RAMCHANDRA DIWAKAR'S VISIT

KING'S INDIA VISIT 10 FEBRUARY TO 10 MARCH 1959

IN MID-AUGUST 1958, the Kings had received an important visitor, Ranganath Diwakar, one of Gandhi's chief lieutenants in the Quit India movement of 1942, and also the author of *Satyagraha*. During interaction with him, they realised that the idea of going to jail would aid their cause. Gandhi had done this in India with good results; King had also started thinking on those lines.

After this three-day visit of Diwakar and his associates, Coretta said, '*We began to think more deeply about the whole philosophy of nonviolence. We talked about how superficial and shallow our knowledge of the whole thing was.*'

The September month unfolded yet another

blood-curdling incident for the Kings, when a mentally deranged woman, Mrs Izola Curry, attacked King with a steel letter opener.

It was while he sat autographing copies of his newly published book, *Stride Toward Freedom*, in a Harlem department store, that this woman rushed toward him, muttering, '*Luther King, I (have) been after you for five years!*', and plunged a sharp, eight-inch, steel letter opener into his chest. Later, at Harlem Hospital, three surgeons took three hours to remove the opener; it was indeed a close shave.

Messages of good will poured in from all over the world. In a press conference from the hospital, King said that he felt no ill will towards Mrs Curry, adding, '*I hope all thoughtful people will do all in their power to see that she gets the help she apparently needs....*' Mrs Curry was later committed to Mattewan State Hospital for being criminally insane.

King left the hospital on 3 October 1958 and returned to Montgomery. Four months of convalescence followed during which King curtailed all his activities, remaining only a symbolic leader for the time being. During this period, a Jewish synagogue in Atlanta was bombed on 12 October 1958, sending shock waves throughout the nation. Even President Eisenhower broke his customary silence and condemned the violence.

On 20 October 1958, Rev Fred L Shuttlesworth, along with twenty other Birmingham Negroes, was arrested for sitting in the *Reserved for Whites* section of two city buses. This was followed by a boycott of the public transport by the end of the month by the black community. In Atlanta, Rev William Holmes Borders launched a boycott resulting in an end to segregated bus seating in January 1959.

King's responsibilities had been curtailed for the time being. Over the past year, he had been thinking of paying a visit to the land of Gandhi. An invitation from Prime Minister Nehru lay unheeded on his desk. In February 1959, he decided that the time was right for visiting India and headed towards New Delhi, which he felt was like a pilgrimage for him.

Are you Martin Luther King?

During the Montgomery boycott, Mahatma Gandhi was the guiding light of the technique for bringing a non-violent social change. So as soon as the victory over bus segregation was won, some of his friends suggested that King should visit India and see for himself what the Mahatma, whom he so admired, had done in India.

One such friend was Lawrence Reddick, who had also written his biography, *Crusader without Violence*, and was chairman of the History department at Alabama State College at that time. He also told him that his true test would come when the people who knew Gandhi would pass judgment upon him and the Montgomery bus boycott.

Thus, the three of them – King, Coretta King and Lawrence Reddick – made up *a sort of three-headed team with six eyes and six ears for looking and listening.* On 3 February 1959, just before midnight, the trio left New York by plane, stopping en-route in Paris and staying with Richard Wright, a friend of Reddick's, with whom they discussed European attitudes on the Negro question.

When they reached Delhi on 10 February 1959, via

a roundabout route, because of a fog, they received a grand reception, and were '*looked upon as brothers with the color of our skins as something of an asset. But the strongest bond of fraternity was the common cause of minority and colonial peoples in America, Africa and Asia struggling to throw off racism and imperialism*'.[2]

He told the reporters who had gathered at the airport, 'to other countries I may go as a tourist, but to India I come as a pilgrim.'

As a child, the entire Orient had held a 'strange fascination' for him – the elephants, the tigers, the temples, the snake charmers, but when he really did make it to India as a young man of thirty, he had 'one of the most concentrated and eye-opening experiences of his life'.

He had numerous discussions with the Indians – journalists, educationists and students – and he had dinner with Prime Minister Nehru, realising that 'India is a tremendous force for peace and non-violence at home and abroad. It is a land where the idealist and the intellectual are yet respected'.

To a reporter's query about the tangible gains of the Montgomery bus boycott, he rejoined, 'Our real victory is not so much the desegregation of buses, as it is a new sense of dignity and destiny.'

The most magnanimous hospitality was showered on them wherever they went. Even in the most unexpected places, people asked him, 'Are you Martin Luther King?'

On 1 March, they flew to Ahmadabad and were taken to Sabarmati Ashram. To their delight, the Gandhians accepted them with open arms. 'They praised our experiment with the non-violent resistance technique at Montgomery. They seemed to look upon it as an outstanding example of the possibilities of its use in western civilisation. To them, as to me, it also suggested that non-violent resistance when planned and positive in action could work effectively even under totalitarian regimes.'

Courtesy: American Centre, New Delhi

The Kings felt they were on hallowed ground and joined some six hundred people, mostly *Harijans* in prayer.

He even came across certain people 'who were sleeping in the same room with the beasts of the field' and to his utter shock, he realised that they were the shunned ones – the *untouchables* – who 'worked hardest, and they were trampled over even by the Indian people themselves'. He also came to know what Gandhi had done to give them their selfhood and self-respect.

He journeyed to Trivandrum in Kerala, where he was supposed to address the students of a school, who were the children of former *untouchables*. In his introduction, the Principal said, 'Young people, I would like to present to you a fellow untouchable from the United States of America.'

Although he was initially shocked by these words, he started thinking about the fact: 'Twenty million of my brothers and sisters were still smothering in an airtight cage of poverty in an affluent society … these twenty million brothers and sisters were still by and large housed in rat-infested, unendurable slums in the big cities of our nation, still attending inadequate schools faced with improper recreational facilities.' And I said to myself, 'Yes, I am an untouchable, and every Negro in the United States of America is an untouchable.' (Sermon at Ebenezer Baptist Church, 4 July 1965.)

Their itinerary was constantly crowded, they lunched with Rajkumari Amrit Kaur, had tea with Dr Servapalli Radhakrishnan, attended receptions in their honour at the Quaker Centre and the Gandhi Smarak Nidhi. He addressed the Delhi University Student Union, exhorting them to put an end to tyranny and prejudice throughout the world through non-violent actions. They met President Rajendra Prasad, and had a memorable walk through the Mughal Gardens. They even travelled all the way to meet Jayprakash Narayan, a major exponent of *Sarvodaya*. At his austere ashram, they were pleasantly surprised to find Japanese scholars and technicians who had come to his centre to study his experiments in decentralised, grass-roots democracy.

Shanti Niketan or the abode of peace was their next destination, where the great poet, Ravindra Nath Tagore, had his ashram. Intensely moved by the choral songs of welcome, and farewell and struck by the internationalism of this tranquil place, he was reminded of Mordecai Johnson's lecture on Gandhi in 1950, which he had delivered in Philadelphia, after his return from the World Pacifist Meeting at *Vishvabharti,* a centre of world cultures. This lecture had put an end to the rampant confusion in King's mind, and he had gone and bought half a dozen books on Gandhi.

In Calcutta, he also met Nirmal Kumar Bose, who had been Gandhi's personal secretary, and others associated with the freedom movement.

In Chennai, they visited many temples and churches, and paid a visit to C Rajagopalachari, whom Gandhi called 'the keeper of my conscience'.

Returning to Delhi, they stopped en-route for a full day of sightseeing in Agra, and the day after returning to Delhi, they spent several hours with Pyarelal Nayar, who had authored many books on Gandhi and the freedom movement.

This four-week *pilgrimage* to India left an indelible impression on their minds, imbuing them with the spirit of Gandhi, which would greatly influence them in the years to come.

He returned to America 'more convinced than ever before that non-violent resistance was the most potent weapon available to oppressed people in their struggle for freedom.... The aftermath of hatred and bitterness that usually follows a violent campaign was found nowhere in India. The way of acquiescence leads to moral and spiritual suicide. The way of violence leads to bitterness in the survivors and brutality in the destroyers. But the way of non-violence leads to redemption and the creation of the beloved community'.

As a result of his India visit, he developed a greater understanding of non-violence and his commitment to achieve freedom for his people through non-violent means became deeper.

'*The spirit of Gandhi was very much alive in India ... The trip had a great impact on me personally. It was wonderful to be in Gandhi's land, to talk with his son, his grandsons, his cousin and other relatives, to share the reminiscences of his close comrades, to visit his ashram, to see the countless memorials for him and finally to lay a wreath on his entombed ashes at Rajghat,*' he remarked later.

On 22 March 1959, in a sermon in Montgomery King said, '*If you ask people in India why is it that Mahatma Gandhi was able to do what he did in India, they will say they followed him because of his absolute sincerity and his absolute dedication. Here was a man who achieved in his lifetime this bridging of the gulf, between the Ego and the Id.*'

Martin Luther King's Itinerary in India

The Kings and Lawrence Dunbar Reddick depart for India and Middle East

King arrives in Bombay

King arrives in New Delhi; holds press conference and meets with Rajkumari Amrit Kaur

King attends reception at Gandhi Smarak Nidhi; meets with Sarvepalli Radhakrishnan and Jawaharlal Nehru

King lunches with J B and Sucheta Kripalani; delivers 'Achievement of Racial Justice in the World Today' to Indian Council of World Affairs in New Delhi

King visits the Samadhi

King has tea with Rajendra Prasad; visits Moghul Gardens; addresses Sarvodaya workers

King lunches with Kaka Kalelkar; addresses Delhi University students

King meets with Averell Harriman

King travels to Patna and Gaya; meets with Zakir Hussain and Sri Krishna Sinha

King visits Buddhist temple; tours Vinoba Bhave's ashram; travels with Jayaprakash Narayan

King travels to Burdwan and Calcutta; speaks at Shantiniketan

King holds press conference in Calcutta; dines with Benjamin and Emily Polk and Nirmal Kumar Bose

King meets with students in

Calcutta; attends meeting

King holds press conference in Madras; addresses meetings; stays at Raj Bhavan

King meets Chakravarti Rajagopalachari and Joint Development Commissioner; visits stone temples at Mahabalipuram

King speaks at Shanti Sena rally; gives address at Gandhigram Rural Institute

King visits villages and Hindu temple in Madurai; attends meeting

King attends E M S Namboodiripad luncheon in Trivandrum; visits Cape Comorin

King tours Trivandrum; attends Legislative Assembly meeting; holds press conference

King meets with B D Jatti in Bangalore

King meets with Jaya Chamaraja Wadiyar in Bangalore; attends cattle show

King attends meeting; sees Shantalal Shah at Bombay airport; tours Mani Bhavan with R R Diwakar

King dines with Shantalal Shah; attends meeting led by G L Mehta at Green's Hotel

King views 'A Voice of India;' meets with Sri Prakasa, Y B Chavan, and Congress Party members; spends time with African students; attends dance recital

King travels to Sabarmati ashram in Ahmadabad; meets with Navajivan Trust associates

King travels to Kishangarh; meets with Vinoba Bhave; lunches with Jayaprakash Narayan

King marches with and interviews Vinoba Bhave

King visits Taj Mahal and Agra Fort; travels to New Delhi

King visits Quaker Centre; attends circus in New Delhi

King meets with Pyarelal Nayyar; dines with G Ramachandran

King meets with U S Embassy representatives; lunches with Rajkumari Amrit Kaur; has tea with Sushila Nayyar

King attends farewell reception at Gandhi Smarak Nidhi

King holds press conference; lunches with Ellsworth Bunker; records message for All India Radio; dines with J B and Sucheta Kripalani

King travels to Karachi, Beirut, Jerusalem, and Cairo en route to New York

Reference material on India trip

Historical Material

From Kaka Kalelkar and Sarojini Nanavati

From Stewart Meacham

To Richard Bartlett Gregg

From G Ramachandran

From Jawaharlal Nehru

'Notes for Conversation between King and Nehru'

Account by Lawrence Dunbar Reddick of Press Conference in New Delhi on 10 February 1959

Farewell Statement for All India Radio

James E Bristol to Corinne B Johnson

Statement Upon Return from India

Palm Sunday Sermon on Mohandas K Gandhi, Delivered at Dexter Avenue Baptist Church

A Walk Through the Holy Land, Easter Sunday Sermon Delivered at Dexter Avenue Baptist Church

To William Stuart Nelson

To Jayaprakash Narayan

To G Ramachandran

'My Trip to the Land of Gandhi'

Courtesy: https://kinginstitute.stanford.edu/encyclopedia/india-trip

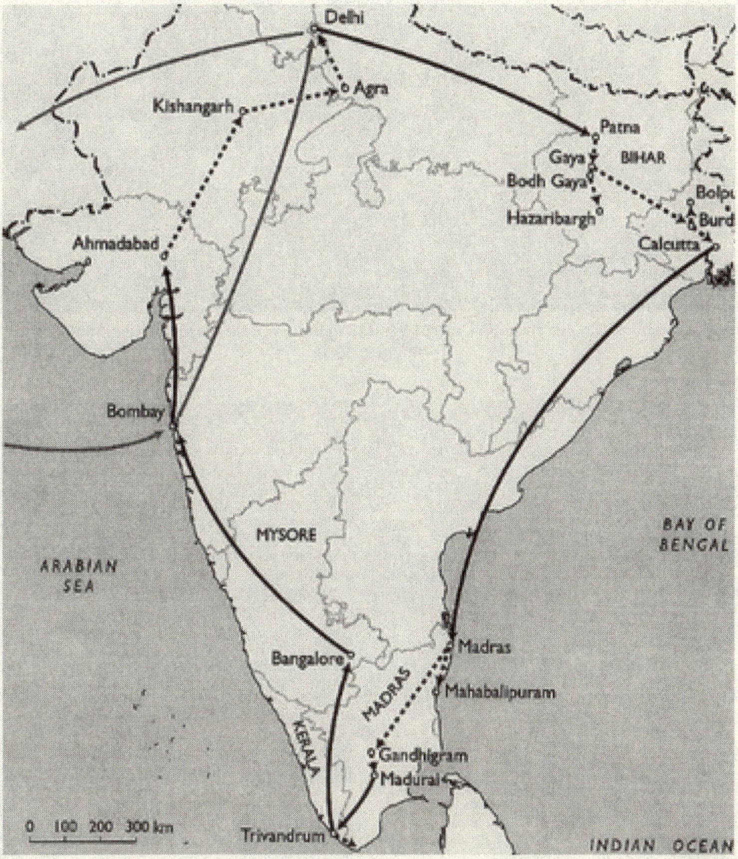

Courtesy: https://maddy06.blogspot.com/2009/10/when-martin-luther-king-jr-visited.html

Martin Luther King Jr and wife Coretta Scott King lay a wreath at Rajghat during a visit to India in 1959

Martin Luther King Jr during a press conference in New Delhi in February 1959

Martin Luther King Jr speaks at the Indian Council of World Affairs during his visit to India in the year 1959

Women and children greet Mrs. King at a reception held in her honor in New Delhi

Martin Luther King at the Quaker Center reception in February 1959

Facsimile of 20 paise stamp the Government of India has issued to honour Martin Luther King Jr

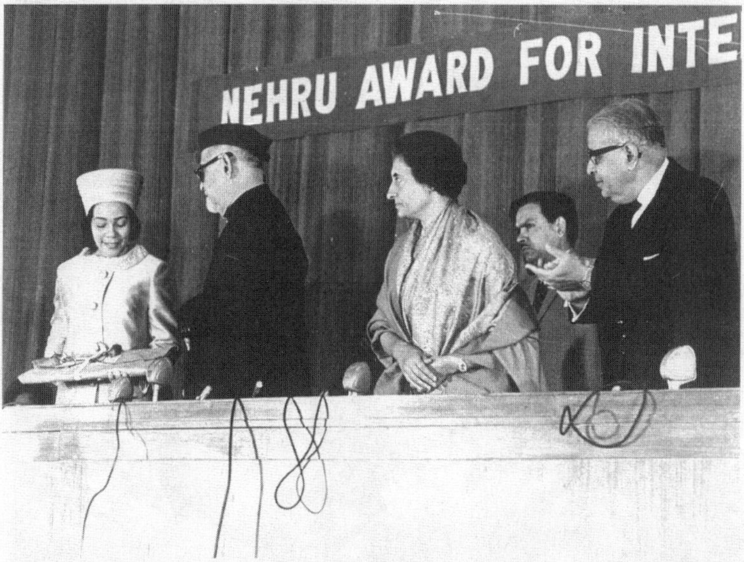

Coretta Scott King, receiving the Jawaharlal Nehru Award for International Understanding for the year 1966 on behalf of her husband, from Dr Zakir Hussain, President of India on 24 January 1969

The stamp being released in honour of King

Coretta Scott King at the Jawaharlal Nehru Award ceremony in1969

Coretta King addressing a public meeting at Gandhi Smarak Nidhi on 22 January 1969
Mrs King presented an album of selected speeches by Martin Luther King Jr on the occasion

Mrs. Coretta King, wife of U.S. civil rights leader Martin Luther King, Jr., looking at the photograph of late Prime Minister Jawaharlal Nehru before receiving the Jawahar Lal Nehru Award for International Understanding for 1966, from Dr. Zakir Hussain, President of India, on January 24, 1969.

All Photographs Courtesy: American Centre, New Delhi

VIOLENCE VS NON-VIOLENCE

BABEL OF VOICES

ALTHOUGH KING returned from his voyage of discovery to India, highly inspired, rested and recuperated, he realised that America's self-discovery was half-hearted, lackadaisical and floundering. White America had hardly begun to realise the all-pervasive malaise that had crept into the white psyche of shunning the blacks, and treating them as inferior. Although nearly five years had elapsed since the Brown vs Board of Education decision, which had paved the way for school desegregation, integration was still not an actual fact. King was afraid that full integration could easily become 'a distant or mythical goal.'

The Civil Rights Act of 9 September 1957 appeared to be a mere pittance on the road to equality. Efforts needed to be redoubled.

Malcolm X vs King

Now there was a new Babel of Voices – voices clamouring for violence, voices clamouring for vengeance, voices demanding that the killers of Mack Parker in Poplaville, Mississippi in

King with Malcom X: Trying to convince him of Gandhian ways

April 1959, in the aftermath of the second Youth March for Integration, be punished. One such voice was of Malcolm X, who rejected appeals to the conscience of white America, criticising King for holding a plea for defencelessness in the face of the 'perfidy of blue-eyed devils'.

Thousands thronged to hear him on the street corners in the black ghettos of the North, where Malcom brutally and persistently castigated the white liberals for their hypocrisy – creating de-facto segregation in schools and other spheres of society. He contended that blacks should use any means necessary to get their freedom and the whites should be prepared for reciprocal bleeding. To him, non-violence was ridiculous and he wondered how blacks could be regarded as human beings if they could not defend themselves.

King, on the contrary, believed that violence was immoral, and was bent on arousing the conscience of the nation. For him, like Gandhi, non-violence did not imply meek submission to the will of the oppressor, but it required great courage. His visit to India had given him a better understanding of the weapon and he was able to proclaim, '*We have a power, power that can't be found in Molotov Cocktails, but we have a power. Power that cannot be found in bullets and guns, but we have a power. It is a power as old as the insights of Jesus of Nazareth and as modern as the techniques of Mahatma Gandhi.*'

It was now being increasingly felt that if the SCLC had to make any tangible advances, an Atlanta-based staff would be required and the president would also have to spend more time there. So bowing before the inevitability of the moment, on 29 November 1959, a tearful King told his congregation at Dexter Avenue Baptist Church that he needed to reorganise his personality and reorient his life, and that history had thrust something upon him that he could not turn away from, and he announced that he would submit his resignation as pastor of Dexter Avenue Baptist Church to become effective on the fourth Sunday in January 1960.

His congregation felt that their pastor was destined for greater goals so they let him go. Now he returned to Atlanta, where the SCLC had established its headquarters, accepting his father's invitation to join him as assistant pastor of Ebenezer Baptist Church.

King was ready to take his beliefs a step farther than he had done in Montgomery. His India trip had solidified his commitment to non-violent direct action. Now he was on the verge of entering new territory. In the first phase in Montgomery, he had been involved in a classic passive resistance action, and no laws were broken. Now the next phase would involve Civil Disobedience. Earlier, they had won by not doing – by refusing to ride the buses, but now they would necessarily 'do' something; they would refuse to obey unjust laws. This was a philosophical leap from passive resistance to Civil Disobedience.

In a press statement the next day, 30 November 1959, which was dated for release on 1 December 1959, King stated, '*The time has come for a bold, broad advance of the Southern Campaign for equality.... We must train our youth and adult leaders in the techniques of social change through non-violent resistance.*'

The *Sit-In Movement*, a little more than a month later, galvanised certain black students into a spontaneous protest against the segregated lunch counters.

On 31 January 1960, Joseph McNeill, a student at the all-black North Carolina Agricultural and Technical College felt great pangs of hunger. On trying to get something to eat at the Greensboro bus terminal's lunch counter, he was brazenly snubbed, '*We don't serve Negroes*', he was told. He and his roommate, Ezell Blair Jr, now undertook their own non-violent protest. Within weeks, a student revolt had been ignited throughout the state. Soon the movement started spreading throughout the South, with the fervour of a holy crusade. By the end of March 1960, these non-violent sit-ins had spread to more than fifty Southern cities. The students now pushed the movement to a new plateau, forging a new generation of black leaders, many of whom went on to become King's trusted teammates later on.

Although King did not initiate this movement, his symbolic

presence was felt throughout, his spirit was very much part of the movement. Some dos and don'ts had been drawn up for these students by John Lewis and Bernard Lafayette, a student of American Baptist Seminary: Don't talk back. Sit up straight. Don't lash out. Don't hit back, remember the teachings of Jesus, of Gandhi, and Martin Luther King Jr.

Student Non-Violent Coordinating Committee (SNCC)

In the initial days, the students were doing everything on the spur of the moment, but then the SNCC came into existence. King wanted to put together a youth leadership conference and, in April 1960, the Student Non-violent Coordinating Committee was born, not as an arm of the SCLC, but as an independent group, with its office in Atlanta. Its members, however, always felt a great affection and love for King.

Throughout the summer, the sit-ins continued. King himself participated in a lunch-counter sit-in against a foremost departmental store in Atlanta, with the result that he was arrested along with other demonstrators. King vowed to 'stay in jail ten years if necessary'. Later, on Senator John F Kennedy's intervention, all the demonstrators were released with the exception of King. He was sentenced to four months of hard labour in Georgia's Public works camps. Taken first to the De Kalb Country Jail, and then transferred three hundred miles from Atlanta to the Reidsville State Penitentiary, he was finally released, thanks again to Kennedy's intervention, on a $2,000 bond on 27 October 1960.

The release of King by the timely intervention of Kennedy, a Democratic presidential candidate, lead Daddy King, a

Republican himself, to endorse his nomination for presidency, and Ralph Abernathy urged blacks to 'take off your Nixon buttons' and the rest is history. Kennedy captured nearly three quarters of the black vote, which played a decisive role in his narrow victory over his Republican rival, Richard Nixon.

During the course of his presidential campaign, Kennedy had reiterated that the President has a responsibility to provide a moral tone and moral leadership in the area of Civil Rights. Kennedy also pledged more vigorous enforcement of the Civil Rights Acts of 1957 and 1960 to protect voting rights, and announced that federally assisted housing could 'be desegregated by the stroke of a presidential pen'.

On 30 January 1961, shortly after the inauguration of Kennedy as the President of the USA, there was another important event in the Kings' life, the birth of their third child, whom they named Dexter Scott, after their beloved Church in Montgomery.

The black Americans had now started hoping that a new, positive chapter in race relations was just round the corner, putting an end to racial discrimination once for all.

Immediately after Kennedy took over the reins of government in 1961, King wrote an article in *The Nation – Equality Now,* urging the new President to undertake 'a radically new approach to the question of civil rights' by sponsoring far-reaching legislation and executive orders to wipe out racial discrimination.

Martin Luther King Jr (2L) with John Kennedy (3R).

The black Americans, who were waiting, with bated breath for the birth of a new era of freedom under the Kennedy administration, were soon to be disappointed, as the Kennedy administration, bowing to the exigencies of the circumstances was now treading cautiously. Procrastinating and beating about the bush, the black demands for the enforcement of the Supreme Court desegregation decisions and a strong Civil Rights Bill, was met with a wary indecisiveness.

Freedom Riders

Confronted with this dilly-dallying of the administration, in March 1961, *CORE* (the Congress for Racial Equality), with the active Support of SCLC and SNCC decided 'to put the sit-ins on the road', to challenge segregation throughout the South, and their destination was New Orleans.

Thus, unfolded a new campaign – the Freedom Riders, which King interpreted as '*the psychological turning point in our legal struggle*'. During these rides, they were lynched, severely beaten with baseball bats and iron pipes, chains and soda crates. The whites who supported them were contemptuously called '*nigger-lovers*' and the blacks were derogatively referred to as a '*bunch of rabble-rousers*' but these valiant warriors did not give up. They were bent on overcoming all obstacles. No Bull Connor* could stop them. Iron pipes and baseball bats could break their skulls, but not their iron determination. Iron was in a head-on collision with iron.

Despite the violence, the Freedom Riders were willing to move on, unfazed. During the course of the movement, Jim Peck, a white, who had fifty stitches from the beatings he received, maintained, '*I think it is particularly important at this time when it has become national news that we continue and show that non-violence can prevail over violence.*'

On 4 May 1961, after President Kennedy was duly informed of their mission, six pairs of black and white volunteers, along

---

* Theophilus Eugene Connor, known as Bull Connor, was an American politician who served as an elected Commissioner of Public Safety for the city of Birmingham, Alabama, for more than two decades. He strongly opposed activities of the American Civil Rights Movement in the 1960s.

with a CORE observer boarded two buses, a Greyhound and a Trailways in Washington D.C. to travel through Virginia, the Carolinas, Georgia, Alabama and Mississippi; the objective being to test the public facilities at each stop, challenging Jim

Crow in terminal restaurants, restrooms and waiting-rooms, and exposing the defiance of federal law throughout the South. The Freedom Riders pledged to remain non-violent, but going a step further, they wanted the federal government to carry out its responsibility towards citizens attempting to exercise their civil rights. As the national director of CORE, James Farmer recalled, '*Their intention was to provoke the Southern authorities into arresting them and prodding the Justice Department into enforcing the law of the land.*'

Although the Supreme Court had outlawed segregation, it still existed openly. In the South, signs still proclaimed *White* and *Colored* in restaurants and waiting-rooms, and on buses. The Freedom Riders wanted to put an end to this unfair segregation.

During the first few days, no untoward incident happened, but when they reached Rock-hill, South Carolina, violence erupted. The Freedom Riders were attacked at the Greyhound Station, when they tried in vain to integrate the *Whites Only* waiting room.

In Alabama, there was still greater violence. When the Greyhound bus reached Anniston on Sunday, 14 May 1961, an irate white mob went on a rampage, puncturing tires and smashing windows. The bus was, however, allowed to depart after the arrival of the police, but now it was chased by cars and an incendiary bomb was thrown at it by the mob. When the Trailways bus arrived in Anniston, the whites again beat up the Freedom Riders, while the police were nowhere to be seen. The same was repeated in Birmingham, where the police stood by, sheathed in impotence.

William Mahoney, a Freedom Rider, remarked, '*At our first stop in Virginia ... I (was) confronted with what the Southern White has called "separate but equal". A modern rest station with gleaming counters and picture-windows was labeled White and a small wooden shack beside it was labeled Colored.*'

Although the Freedom Riders were brutally assaulted, the non-violent protestors adhered to their principles of non-violence, offering no violent resistance. By now, the Freedom Riders had started making national headlines and the media widely circulated the savage assault on them.

The Attorney General, Robert Kennedy, suggested a '*cooling off*' period to the protestors, in view of the violence but they were not to be cowed down by the use of violence, and decided to move on. As James Farmer explained, '*We had been cooling off for a hundred years. If we got any cooler, we'd be in a deep freeze.*'

Outside Birmingham, the bus carrying the riders from Nashville was stopped and, Bull Connor, the Birmingham police chief and, King's most publicised adversary, boarded the bus. They arrested two young men, Paul Brooks, a black, and Jim Swerg, a white, who were then taken to jail.

At the bus station, the bus was virtually taken over by Bull Connor, and saying that they were being taken into protective custody, they were taken to jail instead. From the jail, they were physically lifted, put in the cars, driven to North Alabama and ruthlessly dumped in Klan territory. Given shelter by an elderly couple in a ramshackle cabin, they were later picked up by a driver from Nashville and taken back to Birmingham to continue their journey.

The Freedom Riders got stranded at the Birmingham bus terminal because no bus driver was willing to drive their bus. Ultimately, a driver was found who drove them to Montgomery. The moment they arrived there, they were struck by the all-pervasive peace, which of course, proved deceptive. Suddenly, they sighted people coming from all directions, armed with baseball bats, iron pipes and chains.

The police not being around, the attackers had a field day assaulting the Freedom Riders, with chains and bats. There were no white ambulances available. The violence continued unabated for twenty minutes before the police arrived, who tried to tackle the violence and that too half-heartedly.

Earlier, the Alabama Governor, John Patterson, had declared, '*The people of Alabama are so enraged that I cannot guarantee protection for this bunch of rabble rousers.*' When

Attorney General Kennedy sent nearly seven hundred US marshals, Patterson threatened to arrest them.

King and Ralph Abernathy were horrified when they heard of this ruthless violence. On a speaking assignment in Chicago, they hastened to Montgomery, where Abernathy was the pastor of the First Baptist Church. In a statement, King abhorred the violence, praising the bravery of the young Freedom Riders and suggested a mass meeting to solidify the Montgomery community in support of the Freedom Riders.

One Sunday evening, the Church was filled to capacity and long before 7 pm, a mob came near the Church and started hurling stink bombs and burning cars in front of the Church. The segregationists threw bottles and stones at the Church, and even fought with the US marshals, while more than twelve hundred blacks sang '*we shall overcome*'.

When King arrived at the Church, he exhorted them to be calm and peaceful, and assured them that the President was prepared to act. In undisguised anger, a pained King exclaimed, '*We hear the familiar cry that morals cannot be legislated. This may be true, but behaviour can be regulated. The law may not be able to make a man love me, but it can keep him from lynching me.*'

Finally, on 20 May 1961, Governor Patterson declared martial law and sent national guardsmen to the Church, which was sealed off; King and other blacks were taken to safety. After this, King agreed to serve as the chairman of the *Freedom Rider Coordinating Committee.* He exhorted them '*to develop the quiet courage of dying for a cause*'. The objective of this committee was to fill the jails of Montgomery and Jackson in order to keep a sharp image of the issue before the public.

Unfazed by the ruthless violence, the Freedom Riders, joined by more students, now planned to pass through Mississippi before reaching New Orleans.

On 24 May 1961, twenty-seven Freedom Riders left Montgomery for Jackson and Mississippi in two buses, escorted along the road to Jackson by the Mississippi National Guard and patrol cars, while helicopters and aero-planes flew overhead. The Freedom Riders arrived unscathed in Jackson on 24 May 1961. Immediately on their arrival, they were arrested for attempting to integrate the terminal. The Riders filled the jails, choosing to spend two months there rather than pay the $200 fine.

During these Freedom Rides, King was their symbolic leader. He was greatly pleased that the youth had caught hold of his message and methods. To some, he was a hero; to some, a teacher; and to others, a great source of encouragement, relentlessly prodding the federal government to act more decisively in support of Civil Rights.

Explaining the basis for their non-violent resistance, King said: '*It's a matter of conscience and morality. They must use their lives and bodies to right a wrong. Our conscience tells us that the law is wrong and we must resist, but we have a moral obligation to accept the penalty.*'

On 5 June 1961, King called upon President Kennedy to issue a '*Second Emancipation Proclamation*'.

By now, the Freedom Riders had assumed the proportions of a national movement, continuing to grab the nation's attention throughout the summer of 1961. By the end of the summer, more than 300 people had been arrested in Jackson and more than 1,000 people from different parts of the country had participated in these Freedom Rides.

On 29 May 1961, on King's advice, Attorney General Kennedy formally petitioned the Interstate Commerce Commission (ICC) to act against segregation in inter-state bus terminals. This was followed by an order by the ICC on 22 September 1961, barring segregation in interstate carriers and terminal facilities to be effective from 1 November 1961.

Thus, the Freedom Rides had resulted in substantial gains, instilling a feeling in the blacks that, despite heavy odds, they had emerged victorious. They had really overcome.

James Farmer later reflected that their philosophy was simple, that they put pressure, creating a crisis and then reacted. He was absolutely convinced that the ICC order wouldn't have been issued were it not for the Freedom Rides.

WHEN FAILURE IS SUCCESS

ALBANY, GEORGIA

THE YEAR 1961 saw widespread segregation in the South. The entire justice system was white, and the jails and courts were segregated. The city police – the sheriffs and deputies – all were white. This fifth largest city in the state was a stronghold of racism in the deep South. There were coloured waiting rooms, they drank from coloured water fountains, sat in the coloured parts of buses and had to hunt around for restaurants that would provide food to the blacks.

Diehard supporters of segregation wrote strong articles upholding white supremacy in this city of Georgia, which had a population of around fifty-six thousand people, forty-per cent of them being black. Most Albany blacks were not registered to vote and they had been too apathetic to do anything about the rampant injustice.

In the fall of 1961, Civil Rights agitation began in Albany, Georgia, under the leadership of SNCC. Field workers, Charles Sherrod and Cordell Reagan, established a voter registration drive and also held workshops to initiate blacks in the tactics of non-violence. Spurred on by the efforts of SNCC, Dr William

G Anderson, a black osteopath, formed the Albany Movement, by consolidating a number of local organisations. The goal of the movement was the abolition of segregation in all forms of public facilities within the city.

On 22 November 1961, Police Chief, Laurie Pritchett, arrested five blacks when they tried to integrate a Trailways bus station lunch counter. On 10 December 1961, ten Freedom Riders, including Bernard Lee, the SCLC youth director, were arrested. Talking to the press, Pritchett said that they would not stand for the trouble-makers coming to their city for the sole purpose of disturbing the peace and quiet of Albany. Massive demonstrations followed these arrests, meetings were held in black churches throughout Albany, and more than 500 high school and college students were arrested for parading without a permit.

On 14 December 1961, the protest appeared to be faltering, so Anderson issued a formal invitation to King to speak at a movement meeting. Abernathy and King had been keenly following the course of the events from the SCLC headquarters in Atlanta.

On Friday, 15 December 1961, King arrived with Abernathy and Walker, with no clear cut goals or strategy, but only a hope to revive the sagging movement and inject some vitality in the demoralised blacks.

'Get on your walking shoes: walk together, children, and don't cha get weary', King exhorted the audience of over a thousand who had assembled at Shiloh Baptist Church in Albany on 15 December 1961, while the blacks sang '*we shall overcome*'. During the meeting, Dr Anderson suddenly asked King to lead a protest march to City Hall the next day.

Some activists, however, did not like the intrusion of King and the SCLC at this juncture, when they had already planted the seed. They felt that instead of intensifying the focus of the movement, his presence would only detract from it.

King, Abernathy and Anderson led a procession of 264 marchers to Albany City Hall on 16 December 1961, and they were arrested for parading without a permit. King vowed to remain in jail until the movement's demands were met. Exhorting the blacks throughout the nation to join him in Albany, he promised, '*I will refuse to pay the fine. I expect to spend Christmas in jail and I hope thousands will join me.*'

But two days after his arrest, on 18 December, to the nation's surprise, King was released from jail. This was the outcome of a verbal truce between the movement leaders, Anderson and Marion Page, and the city commissioners. To a skeptical King, Anderson explained that the truce was the '*practical course to take*'. Left with no choice, he accepted release on bail and returned to Atlanta.

In accordance with the truce, a bi-racial committee would work out a schedule for desegregating the city, but alas, there was no desegregation. The movement appeared to have been outmaneuvered by the white power structure and was now on the brink of defeat. An intensely pained King, later remarked, '*I'm sorry, I was bailed out. I did not understand at that time what was happening. We thought that the victory had been won. When we got out, we discovered, it was all a hoax, we had lost an initiative that we never regained.*'

On 27 February 1962, Abernathy and King returned to Albany to stand trial for the 16 December march. Found guilty of disorderly conduct and parading without a permit, however, the sentencing was postponed until 10 July 1962. In the meantime, King embarked on a speaking tour. On the day of sentencing, the judge presented King and Abernathy two alternatives to choose from: A fine of $175 or 45 days in jail. King chose the latter, hoping that this would give the movement the desired publicity inducing federal intervention.

But once again, they were outsmarted by the white authorities. After only three days in jail, on 13 July 1962, Chief Pritchett told them that they were being released because an unidentified well-dressed Negro man had paid their fines. An utterly bewildered Abernathy later exclaimed at a mass meeting: 'I've been thrown out of lots of places in my day, but never before have I been thrown out of jail.'

Among the members of the Albany movement, speculation was rife that the justice department had arranged the release; King surmised that taking a leaf from Commissioner Sellers in Montgomery, Chief Pritchett had himself sent someone to pay the fine. Pritchett later confessed, 'It was a matter of strategy … an arrangement was made.' On 16 July 1962, an unrelenting King announced that their fight was on. Before crowds in Shiloh Baptist and Mount Zion Churches, he thundered to '*turn Albany upside down*'.

On 20 July 1962, Robert Elliot, District Court Judge, a segregationist, restrained them from engaging in unlawful picketing, congregating or marching on the streets, and from 'any act designed to provoke breaches of the peace'. This injunction banned demonstrations till 30 July 1962. Deciding to obey the injunction, they stopped the activities that had created disruption in Albany for the past eight months. However, they continued working vigorously in higher courts to have it dissolved and, eventually, on 24 July 1962, the federal Fifth Circuit Court of Appeals rescinded the injunction of the lower District Court, allowing the resumption of demonstrations after a delay of five days.

Close on the heels of this verdict, violence broke out. The very same evening, about two thousand black youth started pelting bottles and stones at the police in retaliation to an incident a day before, when the pregnant wife of the movement's Vice President, Mrs Slater King, was brutally beaten when she had gone to deliver packages to prisoners in the Mitchell County.

An intensely distraught King, overruling the objections of SNCC, in typical Gandhian style, suspended demonstrations, declaring 26 July 1962, a day of penitence, following it by prayer vigils.

[On 5 February 1922, in Chauri Chaura, a small town

in Gorakhpur District of the United Provinces in India, a violent incident had made Gandhi immensely sad. Some processionists, on reaching a police station, were jeered at by the constables. In angry retaliation, they set that police station on fire, where the constables had taken shelter, causing the death of many constables. Against the advice of his colleagues, Gandhi suspended the non-cooperation campaign saying that such a reversal may be '*politically unsound and unwise, but there is no doubt that it is religiously sound*'. A painful exclamation was wrenched from his heart, '*no provocation can possibly justify brutal murder of men …*' on an individual level; he underwent personal cleansing and fasted for five days.]

As King, Abernathy and Anderson led a prayer vigil in front of City Hall on 27 July 1962, they were again arrested and imprisoned. From his prison, he penned an article for the New York *Amsterdam News* referring to Albany as '*a symbol of segregation's last stand*'. In the meantime, Chief Pritchett complained in a hearing before Judge Elliot that King's presence in Albany had 'raised community tension to the kindling point'.

The movement received an unexpected boost from President Kennedy, when he said in a nationally televised press conference, on 1 August 1962, that he failed to understand why the Albany officials were unwilling to negotiate with the black American citizens when the United States could negotiate with the Soviet Union. Mayor Kelley's rejoinder was that the city would 'never negotiate with outside agitators whose avowed purpose is to create turmoil'.

While King was in jail, an interracial group of clergymen

went to Washington to try to bring about reconciliation by urging federal intervention in Albany, and a bi-partisan group of United States senators also requested the justice department to take all possible steps to assist those imprisoned in the city. King, however, felt that this support of the Kennedy administration could offer no solution to the problems in Albany.

On Friday, 10 August 1962, King and his associates were again tried, for their arrests of 27 July 1962, on the charges of disturbing the peace and parading without a permit. Although convicted, once again in a shrewd tactical move, instead of being jailed, they were given suspended sentences, again losing the opportunity to gain publicity for their movement. A highly disappointed King announced the same evening, the decision to halt demonstrations and spend the weekend in Atlanta.

The city commission's intransigent attitude forced King to return to Albany on 13 August 1962. An intensely frustrated Anderson remarked that the movement would now concentrate on voter registration. Dr Ralph Abernathy rejoined resignedly, '*There comes a time to leave.*'

The Albany Campaign: A failure?

The Albany Campaign was labeled a colossal failure by many Civil Rights leaders and the press. There were no tangible results, and conditions remained the same until the enactment of the Civil Rights Act of 1964. The valiant Freedom Riders never made it to New Orleans – their final destination. Beaten, bruised and battered, many spent their summer in jail; some were permanently scarred from the beatings they received.

Some attributed its failure to the lack of a precise strategy and clear cut goals; some held the friction between the SNCC and SCLC responsible for it. Others believed that the shrewd tactics of Police Chief Laurie Pritchett, of meeting 'non-violence with non-violence', and unlike Bull Connor and Jim Clark, not using fire hoses, clubs, police dogs, but a polite discretion in tackling the crusaders, was responsible for its failure. Later, Pritchett proclaimed triumphantly that they were indeed very proud of the outcome.

Coretta King conceded, '*Police Chief Laurie Pritchett was not at all typical of Southern policemen. He was not brutal, though some of his officers engaged in brutality. He tried to be decent. Our people were given fair warning, often they would refuse to disperse, and would drop on their knees and pray. Chief Pritchett would bow his head with them while they prayed. Then, of course, he would arrest them and the people would go to jail, singing.*'

To a large extent, the crippling tactical moves of the Albany city authorities also put a brake on the movement. Every time King was jailed, he was released prematurely, lest the movement gain unnecessary publicity by his imprisonment. King was jailed thrice, but 'the first time he was lured from jail by a bogus truce between the movement and the city; the second time he was bailed out; and the third time, he received a suspended sentence'.

One more weakness responsible for its failure was their desire to bring about absolute desegregation everywhere. Their focus on many grievances and demands, instead of a couple of targets at a time, proved harmful for the movement. In short, the Albany movement attempted to achieve too much, and without a clear focus, a precise strategy, in too little a time and it was not too easy a task. Despite the failure of the Albany movement, it cannot be denied that it indeed symbolised '*a big beginning in the deep South*'.

America in Dilemma

America was in the midst of a dilemma. On the one hand, was the American constitution, which profoundly proclaimed the equality of its citizens, and on the other hand, there were the blacks who had suffered the crippling and emasculating effects of generations of heartless inequality, oppression and brutalisation.

Through these Freedom Rides, the Freedom Riders tried to prod the American political system to fulfill its ideal of equality and freedom enshrined in the Declaration of Independence, reminding America of its lofty principles. The Albany movement had injected a certain vitality in the SCLC, and SCLC indeed came of age in Albany.

This movement was, however, not an utter failure because they learnt many lessons from it. King was of the opinion that Albany, in fact, proved how extraordinary was the Negro response to the appeal of non-violence. He was to remark later, '*Negroes have straightened their backs in Albany, and once a man straightens his back, you can't ride him anymore.*'

Despite heavy odds, the contribution of the Freedom Riders in the Civil Rights movement cannot be downplayed. In his autobiography, King says: '*In short, our movement had taken the moral offensive, enriching our people with a spirit of strength to fight for equality and freedom even if the struggle is to be long and arduous. The people of Albany had straightened their backs, and as Gandhi had said, no one can ride on the back of a man unless it is bent.*' (Clayborne Carson, Ed, Chapter 16.)

The Negroes of Albany had been living in an atmosphere of silent turbulence, imploding with a highly corrosive low self-esteem. Scarred by the centennial trauma of segregation, their pain had throbbed, unseen. But, the Freedom Riders forged ahead, chest forward, backs straight, holding aloft the banner of non-violence, with fervour, hitherto unseen in Albany. Through it all, they had metamorphosed into giants, who could no longer be silenced, this victory, albeit partial, could not be undone now.

They were on the road to a new beginning, having realised the potential of the weapon of non-violence to defeat tyrants.

'*To the Negro, in the South staggering under a burden of centuries of inferiority, to have faced his oppressor squarely, absorbed his violence, filled the jails, driven his (white) segregated buses off the streets, worshipped in a few white churches, rendered inoperative parks, libraries and pools, shrunken his (white) trade, revealed his (white) inhumanity to the nation and the world and sung, lectured and prayed publicly for freedom and equality.*' (Ed. Clayborne Carson.)

CONFRONTING 'SEGREGATION FOREVER'

BIRMINGHAM AND GEORGE WALLACE

BIRMINGHAM WAS the most segregated city in America. Caught in a Rip Van Winkle sleep, it was the very embodiment of the American dilemma, its intensely racist polices being symbolised by Alabama's Governor, George Wallace, who had pledged in his January 1963 inaugural address: *Segregation Now, Segregation Tomorrow, Segregation Forever.*

Birmingham was not a non-violent city and the blacks here believed in retaliatory violence, because they had been oppressed for long, their manhood had been compromised, their homes had been bombed.

Blatant segregation was rampant in Birmingham. Although the blacks constituted 40 per cent of the Birmingham population of 350,000 only, 10,000 of a total of 80,000 registered voters were black. Confined to mainly menial jobs, there was brazen discrimination in the salary and promotions of the better employed.

Birmingham was said to be the only place on earth where the essential ingredients of iron-making existed in one spot – coal, iron ore and lime, which had proved to be its boon and bane.

This city of dubious superlatives had become impoverished by the Great Depression. Unemployment and illiteracy were rampant and all sorts of diseases had raised their heads. The homicide rate was so high that it was known as the murder capital of the world.

The NAACP had been outlawed in Alabama in 1956. This stirred Rev Fred Shuttlesworth into action, and he organised the *ACMHR – Alabama Christian Movement for Human Rights* in Birmingham in 1956. The rationale behind the movement being that an organisation can be outlawed, but they cannot possibly '*ban a movement in the hearts of American people who are determined to be free*'.

Shuttlesworth, whom King called '*one of nation's most courageous freedom fighters*', had rejoined, '*the fight's on*' even after a dynamite had blown off the roof of his house during the campaign to desegregate the buses. With an indomitable spirit, Shuttlesworth had carried on the non-violent fight against segregation, quietly building a cohesive organisation, laying the groundwork for future progress and for King's entry into Birmingham.

Shuttlesworth had been asking King for starting a joint protest in Birmingham and launching a massive assault upon segregation there. After a series of telephonic conversations with Shuttlesworth in September 1962, SCLC decided to accept his invitation.

'*New Day dawns for Birmingham,*' screamed the headlines of the *Birmingham News* of 3 April 1963. Bull Connor had been defeated by Albert Boutwell in the Mayoral race. In spite of the results of the election, Bull Connor and his two other commissioners reiterated that they could not be removed from office until their term expired in 1965. So, the city was under two governments during the Birmingham confrontation. Connor continued to be Police Chief.

Echoing the viewpoint of Attorney General Robert Kennedy that the new mayor should be given a chance, many supporters maintained that the movement was ill-timed. They argued that, with Albert Boutwell as mayor, things would definitely improve, as he was a moderate segregationist. But King and Shuttlesworth thought differently. For Shuttlesworth, Bull was 'a roaring bull' and Boutwell was 'a crying bull.' He emphasised, '*We've been waiting for 340 years for our rights. We want action. We want it now.*' So, now they launched a well-planned action. Four goals were established for the Birmingham Campaign.

1) The desegregation of lunch counters, fitting rooms, rest rooms and drinking fountains in department stores;
2) The upgrading and hiring of blacks throughout the industrial and commercial community;
3) Amnesty for the demonstrators and
4) Creation of a bi-racial committee to work out a time table for desegregation elsewhere in the city.

Accordingly, Shuttlesworth, King and Wyatt Walker (Executive Director of SCLC) chalked out a battle plan and labeled it Project C, wherein 'C' stood for 'confrontation'.

Mass demonstrations began in Birmingham on 3 April 1963 after a couple of postponements. The demonstrators were requested to participate in rigorous training in non-violence. Each volunteer was required to sign a commitment card which read: '*I hereby pledge myself – my person and body – to the non-violent movement.*' The card mentioned Ten Commandments of non-violent behaviour:

1) Meditate daily on the teachings and life of Jesus;
2) Remember always that the non-violent movement in Birmingham seeks justice and reconciliation – not victory;
3) Walk and talk in the manner of love, for God is love;
4) Pray daily in order that all men might be free;
5) Sacrifice personal wishes in order that all men might be free;
6) Observe with both friend and foe the ordinary rules of courtesy;
7) Seek to perform regular service for others and for the world;
8) Refrain from violence of fist, tongue or heart;
9) Strive to be good in spiritual and bodily health; and
10) Follow the directions of the movement.

The first demonstrations which started on 3 April 1963 were limited to lunch counter sit-ins at the downtown stores. They planned to begin slowly, testing the city's response and then heading towards a gradual escalation in order to provoke a crisis. King had earlier instructed SCLC's Wyatt Walker to '*find some way to create a crisis in Birmingham*'.

Instead of assaulting all forms of segregation, as they had done unsuccessfully in Albany, this time they decided to focus on the downtown Birmingham business community. During the first three days of the movement, Bull Connor made thirty-five arrests. On the night of 5 April 1963 at a mass meeting, King's eloquent words inspired the protestors: '*If I were to seek to give you a blueprint for freedom in Birmingham tonight, I would say first that at this moment we must decide that we will no longer spend our money in businesses that discriminate against Negroes*'.

On 6 April 1963, a group of carefully selected demonstrators marched on City Hall and no sooner had they reached there, they were asked to disperse. When they refused to comply, forty-two marchers were arrested for parading without a permit and quietly escorted to paddy wagons, while the enthusiastic black supporters sang freedom songs.

On 7 April 1963, Bull Connor was provoked into attacking the crowd with clubs and police dogs, which got the movement the publicity that they were waiting for. A group of twenty-five demonstrators headed by AD King, younger brother of Martin Luther King Jr, encountered police dogs. Violence ensued, in which some spectators were also attacked by clubs and dogs.

The movement started gaining greater momentum as the days progressed, and the Easter Boycott began to hurt the downtown business community. Now Connor, deciding to move from the streets into the courts, secured a court injunction barring further demonstrations. But this time, King and the SCLC were taking no chances. They had already planned the course of action for dealing with such an eventuality, one month earlier, at Harry Belafonte's apartment in New York. They were in no mood to obey an order which was '*an unjust, undemocratic and unconstitutional misuse of the legal process*'. King, conferring with his lawyers, had decided that he would defy it as an act of civil disobedience accepting the legal penalty for contempt of court.

The famous singer Harry Belafonte at the protest.

Thus, for the first time, civil disobedience and the non-violent movement merged. In a press conference on 11 April 1963, King declared that they were violating the Alabama State Court injunction '*not out of any disrespect for the law but out of the highest respect for the law*'. SCLC was now all set to follow the Gandhian principles of filling the jails. Ralph Abernethy told a reporter, '*Tell 'em we're going to rock this town like it has never been rocked before*'. King maintained that '*It's better to go to jail with dignity than to accept segregation in humility*'.

King decided to carry out his civil disobedience on Good Friday, 12 April 1963. On this day, about a thousand blacks lined the streets, singing '*we shall overcome*', while King and Abernathy headed a group of fifty-three marchers from Zion Church toward downtown Birmingham. They had hardly marched eight blocks when Bull Connor ordered his men to arrest them. Arrested for the thirteenth time for the cause of Civil Rights, this news was splashed all over the national newspapers.

It was in the claustrophobic confines of the jail cell, that he composed the famous '*Letter from Birmingham Jail*', presenting one of the most articulate and compelling justifications for civil disobedience and direct action. Andrew Young called the letter the turning point in the movement. It was a '*well-stated, well-articulated statement that people can rally around*'.

Letter from Birmingham Jail

'*I am in Birmingham because injustice is here ... injustice anywhere is a threat to justice everywhere.*' These words of King written on the margins of newspapers in the Birmingham Jail, which later became the famous letter from Birmingham Jail, was a rejoinder to eight Alabama clergymen who had drafted a public statement to King, leveling many allegations on him and the movement. These clergymen felt that the movement was lead 'by outsiders', that it was 'unwise and untimely', and they even exhorted King to wait. 'When rights are consistently denied, cause should be pressed in the courts and in negotiations among local leaders and not in the street,' they wrote self-righteously.

Through this letter, King prodded the conscience of America, maintaining that the achievement of Civil Rights for blacks would also imply the fulfillment of the American Dream.

He wrote, '*We will reach the goal of freedom in Birmingham, and all over the nation, because the goal of America is freedom.*' Dated 16 April 1963, this letter was a synthesis of ideas King had been developing for many years.

In the jail, King was initially placed in solitary confinement and not permitted to make any telephone calls even to his attorney or Coretta for more than twenty-four hours.

On Monday, 15 April 1963, a crestfallen Coretta, who had only two weeks before given birth to their fourth child, Bernice Albertine, on 28 March 1963, tried to call President Kennedy. Only minutes later, she received a reassuring call from Attorney General Robert Kennedy, the President's brother, followed by a call from the President himself a few hours later who said he would look into the matter personally. True to his word, King was allowed to call home immediately.

On 20 April 1963, King and Abernathy were released from Birmingham jail after spending eight days in jail and after Harry Belafonte furnished the required amount of $50,000 toward their bail.

And now came another turning point in the movement – the Children's Crusade.

CHILDREN'S CRUSADE FOR FREEDOM

THROUGH THIS children's crusade, SCLC and King were able to heighten the impact of the desegregation movement. Although many detractors condemned King for risking children's lives, calling it a dangerous ploy, SCLC felt that it would enhance the drama of the protest and hasten the progress of the entire Civil Rights campaign. As it is, children would often accompany their parents to the meetings and listen to them talking about freedom and mapping out future strategies.

It was James Bevel, one of the most competent strategists of SCLC, who advised King to involve black children in the movement. Bernard Lee, Dorothy Cotton and Andrew Young visited high schools and local colleges, motivating the students and inviting them to attend mass meetings and non-violent training sessions.

After undergoing rigorous training in the methods of non-violence, an army of young non-violent warriors were all set to launch a non-violent assault on the city of Birmingham on Thursday, 2 May 1963, termed as the D-Day. Fired with a revolutionary fervour, these young soldiers, ranging in age between six and sixteen, set out from the Sixteenth Street Baptist Church singing freedom songs, as the nation watched in speechless wonder.

As Shuttlesworth recollected later, '*Once I saw the waves of children going downtown, and the police couldn't handle it, I knew that the victory was won.*'

Millions of eyes were riveted on the click-clack of young feet as they marched forward, songs on their lips, a glow on their faces, and hope in their hearts. Although accusations were hurled at King, he maintained that it was one of the wisest moves they had made, bringing a new impact to the crusade, and the impetus to win the struggle. '*We wanted to get the nation involved in Birmingham, and to get a larger segment of Birmingham involved. We knew if the students were involved, the parents would come out to find out what was going on.*'

Now, the Birmingham campaign reached a climax. In the initial phase of the campaign, Bull Connor, emulating the policy of Police Chief Laurie Pritchett, had tried to tackle non-violence with non-violence, but the sight of these children marching and singing, pushed the irate Bull Connor beyond the limits of his endurance and he finally struck.

On 3 May 1963, which King had proclaimed as Double D-Day, Connor ordered police to bar the door when almost a thousand black children jammed the Sixteenth Street Baptist Church.

Kelly Ingram Park, across the street, teemed with restive onlookers and demonstrators, while foremen with high pressure hoses and police with ferocious dogs and clubs waited for orders. All of a sudden, there was a commotion. Some of the children who had been trapped in the Church, succeeded in escaping from the Church, and merged with the crowd. '*Let 'em have it!,*' Connor thundered and the police charged on the crowd with blood-curdling cruelty.

Pictures of dogs biting children were splashed all over the newspapers on the morning of 4 May 1963. A wave of indignation rocked the nation, and anguished people watched on their television sets, as Bull Connor perpetrated horror upon unimaginable horror. Prostrated black women were clubbed by policemen; others were blasted by high-pressure hoses. Violence continued, while George Wallace, the Alabama Governor, promised to take strict action to preserve law and order. Needless to say, what he intended to preserve were Alabama's segregation laws.

The barbarities perpetrated by Connor and his men were instrumental in uniting the nation together. As a wave of outrage swept across the world, the Kennedy administration tried to bring about a truce but King was adamant that, '*If the White power structure of this city will meet some of our minimum demands, we will consider calling off the demonstrations, but we want promises plus action.*'

Kennedy likewise took immediate action and the head of the Civil Rights division of the Justice Department, Burke Marshall, was dispatched as a representative of the President to carry out the negotiations.

King and his colleagues were positive that they would soon break down the barriers of segregation. Even while the negotiations were going on, demonstrations were in full swing. Fired by an unprecedented zeal, the non-violent warriors were filling the jails, and the police were creating concentration areas and holding pens to accommodate the crusaders.

King remarked, '*I'm sure we've had more people to give their witness to freedom by going to jail here in Birmingham than in any city in the United States.*'

While the jails were bursting with the non-violent warriors, a furious Bull Connor remarked on 8 May 1963, 'We have just started to fight, if that's what they want. We were trying to be nice to them, but they won't let us be nice.' Needless to say, by this time, the entire world knew what Bull Connor's definition of being 'nice' was. Vicious dogs, high-powered hoses, derogatory words and other highly revolting barbarities were inflicted on innocent people. On 4 May 1963, *New York Times* editorial condemned the atrocities and said that they were '*revoltingly reminiscent of totalitarian excesses*'.

Faced with such a public outcry against the excesses, the federal government had no alternative but to intervene, as Robert Kennedy said, 'Continued refusal to grant equal rights and opportunities to Negroes makes increasing turmoil inevitable.'

Frantic negotiations were now underway. Attempts were made to persuade the black leaders to moderate their demands and the cooperation of Birmingham's industrial and business community was sought. Moreover, secret negotiations between prominent businessmen and black leaders were also on. On 7 May 1963, Fred Shuttlesworth was injured while trying to calm a violent crowd.

Bull Connor now appealed to Governor George Wallace to send troops to Birmingham. Accordingly, Wallace dispatched more than 800 state troopers. The Birmingham merchants were incurring heavy losses due to the economic boycott. Efforts for negotiations became more vigorous, and as a goodwill gesture, King and his colleagues called a 24-hour truce. Eventually, after weeks of demonstrations, an accord was reached on

10 May1963, which emphasised that the city's downtown eating facilities, restrooms and drinking fountains would be desegregated; blacks would be hired on a non-discriminatory basis by business and industry; and a permanent bi-racial committee would be established within two weeks.

The protestors had also moderated their demands. So, instead of complete amnesty for all jailed demonstrators, they were released on bail. Instead of immediate desegregation, there would be gradual implementation, within a specific time frame.

On 10 May 1963, Fred Shuttlesworth, having recovered from his injuries, read a statement to the press announcing the terms of the settlement, and King said, '*I am very happy to be able to announce that we have come today to the climax of a long struggle for justice, freedom, and human dignity in the city of Birmingham ... we must now move from protest to reconciliation.*'

The settlement was praised by Attorney General Robert Kennedy as '*a tremendous step forward for Birmingham, for Alabama, and for the South, generally*'. Hardly had the settlement been reached when violence erupted, giving rise to the speculation that the settlement would be annulled.

King returned to Atlanta on Saturday, 11 May 1963, to be with his family and also to preach at the Ebenezer Baptist Church. The same evening white racists bombed SCLC headquarters in Room 30 of Gaston Motel and also the home of AD King, Martin Luther's brother.

Retaliatory violence followed, when the blacks stormed the downtown Birmingham streets battling with the police. At the Sunday service at Ebenezer, King had said, '*We have some difficult days ahead.... Tied up in the solution of this problem is the very destiny of the nation. And if this is not solved, I am convinced that America is doomed and she will lose her moral and political voice because she failed to live up to the great dream of America.*'

King hastened back to Birmingham on Sunday, and further rioting on the streets was stemmed by his presence.

Now, President Kennedy publicly commended the justness of the Birmingham protest on Mother's Day, and assured the blacks that he had every intention of protecting the agreement. He said '*The Birmingham agreement was and is a fair and just accord. It recognises the fundamental right of all citizens to be accorded equal treatment and opportunity....*' He ordered 3,000 federal troops to the outskirts of the city, and also prepared to federalise the Alabama National Guard.

Pool Room and Other Movements

King and the staff members of the SCLC now set out on a *Pool Room Pilgrimage.* He and Abernathy went into pool halls and bars, and beseeched the young blacks who were not part of the movement to steer clear of violence.

Twentieth May 1963 was a historic day for the non-violent crusaders, for on this day, the United States Supreme Court ruled that Alabama's segregation laws were unconstitutional.

Another victory was just round the corner. Three days later, the Alabama Supreme Court ruled that Boutwell's administration was the sole legitimate government in Birmingham, and Bull Connor and the two other city commissioners had no legitimate right to remain in office.

Through Project 'C', King had prodded the conscience of

America; shaming it into waking up to the rampant injustice entrenched in the American society, despite lofty proclamation to the contrary.

Praising the relevance of King's method, Marshall remarked, '*I think that they were fitted to the times and the problem. Nothing else would have worked. I think he was absolutely right. The path of nonviolence; ... all of that business of a combination of extraordinary bravery and extraordinary passivity at the same time was exactly right.*'

On 11 June 1963, two black students, Vivian Malone and James Hood tried to register at the University of Alabama. George Wallace, the Alabama Governor, carrying out a 1962 campaign promise '*to stand in the school-house door*' literally stood in front of Foster Auditorium, trying to prevent integration. This became known as the '*stand in the school-house door*'. He stood aside only when confronted by federal marshals, Deputy Attorney General Nicholas Katzenbach and the Alabama National Guard. Later, the same day, Wallace withdrew, allowing the students to register.

Vehemently against desegregation of the state of Alabama, he remarked, '*the President wants us to surrender to Martin Luther King ...*' Wallace had been elected Governor in a landslide victory in 1962. He took the oath of office on 14 January 1963, and in his inaugural speech he thundered a threat:

'In the name of the greatest people that have ever trod the earth, I draw the line in the dust and toss the gauntlet before the feet of tyranny, and I say segregation now, segregation tomorrow segregation forever.' [These lines were written by Asa Earl Carter, an outspoken segregationist and the head of the Ku Klux Klan, who had been his main speech writer in the 1962 election.]

In a nationally televised address the same day, the President proclaimed, almost paraphrasing King's ardent belief that '*A threat to justice anywhere is a threat to justice everywhere*':

> The rights of every man are diminished when the rights of one man are threatened.
>
> We are confronted primarily with a moral issue.... Now the time has come for this nation to fulfill its promise. The events in Birmingham and elsewhere have so increased the cries for equality that no city or state legislative body can choose to ignore them.
>
> We preach freedom around the world and we mean it. We cherish our freedom here at home, but are we to say to the world – and much more importantly to each other – and this is the land of the free, except for Negroes, that we have no second class citizens, except for Negroes; that we have no class or caste system, no ghettos, no master race, except with respect to Negroes.

With a passionate eloquence, President Kennedy proclaimed '*that race has no place in American life or law*'.

Thus, the indefatigable crusade of the non-violent warriors spearheaded by the untiring Martin Luther King Jr had finally reaped benefits. King telegraphically acknowledged Kennedy's speech as '*one of the most eloquent, profound and unequivocal pleas for justice and the freedom of all men ever made by any president*'.

In the following week, Congress was asked to pass the most far-reaching Civil Rights Bill ever proposed by a President. It would be a year later, on 2 July 1964 that King and other Civil Rights leaders would be invited by President Johnson to the White House, to watch him sign this historic bill into law.

Regarding the President's proposal, Burke Marshall explained that '*he did it because the country just had to have it, it was because of the efficacy of the Civil Rights movement and especially the work of Martin King*'.

THE MARCH TO WASHINGTON

28 AUGUST 1963

ON 7 JUNE 1963, the Masonic Temple in Jackson was choc-a-bloc for a NAACP rally.

'*It's not enough just to sit there tonight ... And clap your hands and shed your tears and sing and then go out and do nothing about this struggle. Freedom has never been free ... There is something for everybody to do,*' thus spoke Medgar Evers, who had become Mississippi's first field secretary of NAACP in 1954. He was an unassuming, but indefatigable fighter in an atmosphere of high racial tension, where racial discrimination had been institutionalised by the Jim Crow laws. It was this tenacious fight against racial segregation that cost him his life.

'*I love my children, and I love my wife with all my heart. And I would die, and die gladly if that would make a better life for them.*'

Jackson, Mississippi, Midnight 11-12 June 1963

A tired Medgar Evers headed home from a meeting at the New Jerusalem Baptist Church, while his family watched a televised speech by Kennedy, which he had delivered from his

Oval Office – a speech which had lasted thirteen minutes and twenty-four seconds. Talking of the black children, Kennedy said, '*I think we owe them and we owe ourselves a better country than that. We preach freedom around the world and we mean it … Are we to say to the world, and much more importantly, to each other, that this is the land of the free, except for the Negroes?*'

An assassin lurked in the honeysuckle bushes surrounding Evers' home. As he parked his car outside his small house in a black subdivision in Jackson, his family's ears pricked to the crunch of gravel outside. The familiar footfall of an exhausted husband, doggedly pursuing his crusade against the notorious Jim Crow laws; a doting father dreaming dreams of a desegregated world for his three children.

'Here comes daddy,' cried Darrell, the elder son. The excited children rose up to greet him – their father was back after a grueling day. But suddenly, gun shots shattered the nocturnal stillness.

It was in 1954 that the Supreme Court in its landmark Brown versus Board of Education judgement had struck down segregation in schools.

The valiant Civil Rights activist, who would have turned 38 on 2 July 1963, and who, just ten days ago, had been called the 'quiet integrationist' by *The New York Times*, had now turned really quiet – a life throbbing with dreams for his brethren, his family, and his country had been snuffed out by an ardent segregationist, Byron de la Beckwith.

His assassination came just a few hours after President Kennedy's address on Civil Rights, the televised version of which his family sat watching that night, dreams rippling in their eyes, hope taking birth in their hearts. Alas, for Darrell and his siblings, the *better country* that Kennedy promised was not to be. Another mocking bird had been killed senselessly.

'*Nothing can bring Medgar back, but the cause can live on*', Myrlie Evers, Medgar's widow, said to a crowd of nine-hundred people, her face streaked with tears, her heart heavy with sorrow.

Born on 2 July 1925, in Decatur, Mississippi, and having served in the US Army in Europe in World War II, this Civil Rights activist, diligent and competent, had raised the heckles of the segregationists by his advocacy of Civil Rights, organising sit-ins, major voter registration campaigns, advocating boycott of businesses run by racists, fighting the case of Emmett Till, the fourteen-year-old black accused of having raped and murdered a white teenage girl. He had been receiving many threatening telephone calls, and just a few weeks prior to his assassination, a Molotov cocktail had been hurled at his house, through a window, and a car had also injured him.

Medgar was buried with full military honours in Arlington National Cemetery, and was conferred with the 1963 Spingarn Medal of the NAACP.

An intensely pained King said that all persons of good will must be more determined than ever before to break down the barriers of racial segregation and discrimination.

The March for Jobs and Freedom

In the path of their struggle, many a civil rights activist was killed, but the cause had to move on. Life had to move on. The March on Washington, on 28 August 1963, was a landmark march in the black freedom struggle – the finest moment of the non-violent crusade. As James Baldwin said, '*That day, for a moment, it almost seemed that we stood on a height, and could see our inheritance. Perhaps we could make the kingdom real, perhaps the beloved community would not forever remain that dream one dreamed in agony.*'

Firmly convinced that only through the method of non-violence could the blacks win their fight against racial segregation, King was afraid that the ideological extremism of black nationalism would be suicidal for their cause, leading to a frightening racial nightmare. Despite the claims of Malcolm X that the Birmingham campaign was an exercise in futility, and they had gained nothing but a chance to sit at a lunch counter and drink some coffee, the fact was that in the aftermath, thousands of hotels, schools, restaurants, parks and swimming pools had been desegregated. The Birmingham victory had been followed by 758 Civil Rights demonstrations in

186 cities. The time was ripe for another assault on the American conscience.

Now, King joining forces with the heads of *CORE, SNCC, NAACP*, the Urban League and white labour leaders, planned a massive march on Washington.

On 22 June 1963, some of the leaders met President Kennedy, who was apprehensive that the march could be ill-timed and counterproductive. But King rejoined, '*Frankly, I have never engaged in any direct action movement, which did not seem ill-timed... some people thought Birmingham ill-timed.*' Ultimately, when it appeared that the march was unavoidable, the Kennedy administration was also supportive of it.

On 23 June 1963, King spearheaded a great Freedom Walk in Detroit, leading 125,000 people. Introduced as America's '*beloved freedom fighter*', King called the event '*the largest and greatest demonstration for freedom ever held in the United States*'.

This Freedom March was almost like a rehearsal for the main event to the Northern capital on 28 August 1963, demonstrating that 'Birmingham tells us something in glaring terms. It says first that the Negro is no longer willing to accept racial segregation in any of its dimensions, as segregation is a cancer in the body politic'.He said further, '*We are through with segregation now, henceforth, and forever.*'

There was an ear-splitting applause as Randolph introduced King as '*the moral leader of the nation*'. Thousands of people witnessed the historic event on television and radio, hanging on to every word.

Many more roared as the charismatic dreamer approached the rostrum. Then a silence fell. King's powerful baritone swept across the audience, as Abraham Lincoln looked on in statuesque contemplation. The atmosphere almost had a festive fervour, there were blacks who had come to Washington for the first time, their faces glowing in the sweltering heat; they unpacked their picnic hampers and looked around at the lawns and at the memorial with a proprietorial attitude. There was a whiff of something momentous hanging in the air. Blacks holding placards which boldly proclaimed:

> WE SEEK THE FREEDOM IN 1963, PROMISED IN 1863 NO U.S. DOUGH TO HELP JIM CROW
>
> Five score years ago, a great American, in whose symbolic shadow we stand today, signed the emancipation proclamation… but one hundred years later, the Negro is still not free.
>
> When the architects of our republic wrote the magnificent words of the constitution and the declaration of

Independence, they were signing a promissory note to which every American was to fall heir. This note was the promise that all men – yes, black men as well as white men – should be guaranteed *the unalienable rights of life, liberty and the pursuit of happiness.*

Toning down his original speech, which some of the Civil Rights activists said, could be inflammatory, John Lewis delivered an emotionally surcharged speech, which moved the audience. '*We are tired! We are tired of being beaten by policemen. We are tired of seeing our people locked up in jail over and over again! And then you holler "be patient". How long can we be patient? We want our freedom and we want it now.*'

On the day of the march, James Farmer was in Louisiana jail, but his message was read by Floyd McKessick, his colleague from CORE: '*We will not stop until the dogs stop biting us in the South and the rats stop biting us in the North.*'

New York Senator, Jacob Javits, remarked that the march ill certainly establish a mood for the coming Civil Rights ongressional battle. King also said: '*The march has already ne great deal to create a coalition of concern about the status of l rights in this country. It has aroused the conscience of millions eople to work for this legislation.*'

King's impassioned oratory, an inspiring combination of emporaneous verve, and a heartfelt eloquence was hailed of the most moving orations of the times. Definitely well-reasoned legal brief on the Civil Rights bill, nor an ual treatise on the plight of blacks in America, this was emotional appeal to the comatose conscience of a mélange of the democratic spirit and Christianity,

combined with his powerful baritone, and his incredible charisma, it was able to lift commonplace truisms to the level of a divine rule.

For King, this peaceful and orderly march was a vindication of his philosophy of non-violence. It not only united the black leaders of different organisations, irrespective of their differing ideologies and goals, it also symbolised the participation of whites in the black movement.

Death of four little girls

Hardly had the euphoria over the success of the Freedom March to Washington died down, hardly had the significance of King's dream sunk into peoples' minds, hardly had his inspiring oratory been hailed as one of the most moving speeches of the times, hardly had the resonance of the words, '*I have a dream that my four little children will one day live in a nation where they will be judged not by the colour of their skin, but by the content of their character*', stopped ringing, than a nightmare unfolded snuffing out the lives of four other little children!

On the morning of 15 September 1963, a bomb exploded during Sunday school in Birmingham's Sixteenth Avenue Baptist Church, smashing the dreams of four little girls, as they were putting on their choir robes!

The nation was stunned. An appalled King said, '*Never in Christian history within a Christian country have Christian churches been on the receiving end of such naked brutality, and violence as we are witnessing here in America today. Not since the days of the Christians in the catacombs has God's house as a symbol weathered such an attack as the Negro churches.*'

This tragedy occurred in the wake of tumultuous efforts to integrate schools in Alabama, many people, including King, put the blame on George Wallace, who had vehemently opposed school desegregation and had thundered a threat in his inaugural speech as Governor of Alabama.

Seething in anger, King said, '*Certainly the Governor of Alabama has to take a great deal of the responsibility for this evil act, for his defiant, irresponsible words and actions have created the atmosphere for violence and terror all over the state.... And the murders of yesterday stand as blood on the hands of Governor Wallace.*'

THE ASSASSINATION OF PRESIDENT KENNEDY

ON 22 NOVEMBER 1963, President John F Kennedy was assassinated in Dallas, Texas, plunging the entire nation into deep and utter sorrow. President Kennedy, the 35th president of the USA, before he died had laid down the outlines of the reforms that would go on to become the most sweeping legislation of social justice.

Towards the end of 1963, President Kennedy and his advisers had started preparing for the next presidential campaign. On 21 November 1963, the President and the First Lady departed for a two-day five-city tour of Texas and on 22 November 1963, just before 12:30 pm CST, as their car passed the Texas School Book Depository, there was the sudden reverberation of gunfire at Dealey Plaza.

President Kennedy slumped over towards Mrs Kennedy; bullets had struck his head and neck. Texas Governor, John Connolly, and his wife, Nellie, were also sitting in the open convertible. The former was hit in the chest. Though seriously wounded, he survived.

The car dashed towards Parkland Memorial Hospital, just

a stone's throw away. But Kennedy, who had just some time back, during breakfast, said, '*We will continue to do ... our duty,*' was declared dead at 1:00 pm, his desire to do his duty cut short.

Lee Harvey Oswald, a recently hired employee of the Texas School Book Depository, was arrested for the killing. But, on 24 November, he was killed by Jack Ruby, a local night club owner.

King sat upstairs in his Atlanta home in a distracted state, trying to make preparations for a Los Angeles fund raising appearance, absentmindedly listening to a programme on the television when he suddenly sat upright. There was a special bulletin, which stated that President Kennedy had been seriously wounded. King was dumbfounded. Bernard Lee and Coretta, who were downstairs came up, and the grief-stricken threesome huddled before the television set hoping and praying for a miracle, which was not to be. Shortly after 2:30 pm, utterly devastated, they listened to the news of the death of the thirty-fifth President of the United States.

The pain in the air was palpable. A heartbroken King turned to Coretta and said, '*I don't think I'm going to live to reach forty.*'

'Don't say that Martin', a cry was wrenched from Coretta's heart.

'*This is what is going to happen to me also. I keep telling you, this is a sick nation. And I don't think I can survive either.*' King was adamant.

Eight-year-old Yolanda King arrived home from school, tear-stricken. 'Oh Daddy, now we will never get our freedom,' she moaned, flinging herself into her father's arms. 'Now don't you worry, baby, It's going to be all right,' King, said, soothingly.

Six-year-old Marty asked, 'Daddy, President Kennedy was your best friend, wasn't he, Daddy?'

Bernice and Dexter were too small to understand the grief that the nation had been plunged into, even Yoki and Marty were not old enough to comprehend the colossal loss to the country, but King knew that he really had lost a friend, who, after a three-year-long clash of views with him, had finally been won over to their way of thinking. He had finally seen their problem in all its dimensions, and conceded that '*this nation for all its hopes and boasts will not be fully free until all its citizens are free*'.

Kennedy, King said, '*had tried to rid our nation of the vestiges of racial segregation and discrimination*'.

Earlier, on 11 June 1963, Kennedy had mentioned that the question of race was neither a sectional issue nor a partisan issue. It was not even a legislative issue, but a moral issue.

> The Negro baby born in America today, regardless of the section of the nation in which he is born, has about as much a chance of completing high school as a white baby born in the same place on the same day, one-third as much chance of completing college, one-third as much chance of becoming a professional man, twice as much chance of becoming unemployed, about one-seventh as much chance of earning $ 10,000 a year, a life expectancy which is seven years shorter, and the prospects of earning only half as much.

An intensely pained King said,

> Our late President was assassinated by a morally inclement climate. It is a climate filled with heavy torrents of false accusation, jostling winds of hatred and raging storms of violence. It is a climate where men cannot disagree without being disagreeable, and where they express their dissent through violence and murder.

In his first presidential address to Congress, less than a week after taking office, the thirty-sixth President of the US, Lyndon B Johnson said, '*No memorial or eulogy could more eloquently honour President Kennedy's memory than the earliest possible passage of the Civil Rights Bill for which he fought so long.*'

Encouraged by Johnson's positive stance on the Civil Rights question, King told a *Time* reporter, '*I have implicit confidence in this man ... we have in the White House a man, who is deeply committed to help us.*'

BOUQUETS AND BRICKBATS

IN ITS 3 January 1964 issue of *Time* Magazine, Martin Luther King Jr was named 'Man of the Year' for 1963, the first black American to receive this honour. He was featured on its cover, and the magazine announced that he was chosen not only '*as a man, but also as a representative of his people for whom 1963 was perhaps the most important year in their history.*' It also stated '... *Few can explain the extraordinary King mystique, yet he has an indescribable capacity for empathy that is the touchstone of leadership. By deed and by preachment, he has stirred in his people a Christian forbearance that nourishes hope and smothers injustice.*'

In the January SCLC newsletter, King wrote, '*If the Bill were not passed, the nation might well fasten its safety belt.*'

In the March SCLC newsletter, King declared that the Bill was '*so critical for the domestic health of our national community that we must mobilise every force and pressure available to see to it that the Civil Rights Bill before the senate gets through, as it is.'*

King receives the Nobel Prize

As the new year dawned on the horizon, friction between SNCC and SCLC continued, but King reached the height of his prestige, emerging, by the end of 1964, as the undisputed leader of the blacks, notwithstanding a few discordant voices, which continued to heap venom at him.

In July 1963, a *Newsweek* magazine poll showed that he had an eighty-eight per cent approval rating among the black rank-and-file, and ninety-five per cent among the black leadership. His national stature touched new heights with the passage of the Civil Rights Act of 1964. At the age of 35, in October 1964, King became the youngest recipient in the history of the Nobel Peace Prize to be chosen for the Award.

On 10 December 1964, Mr Gunnar Jahn, Chairman of the Nobel Prize Committee, delivered a speech in the auditorium of the University of Oslo, saying:

> Today we pay tribute to Martin Luther King, the man who has never abandoned his faith in the unarmed struggle he is waging, who has suffered for his faith, who has been

imprisoned on many occasions, whose home has been subjected to bomb attacks, whose life and the lives of his family have been threatened, and who, nevertheless, has never faltered. To this undaunted champion of peace, the Nobel Committee of the Norwegian Parliament has awarded the peace prize for the year 1964.

King termed the award as a recognition of non-violence as an answer to the crucial political and moral question of the time and the need for man to overcome oppression and violence without resorting to violence and oppression.

Although there was jubilation among a large portion of black Americans, there was no dearth of detractors, like Herbert Hoover, the FBI Head, who seethed in anger on hearing the news.* He had every intention of sabotaging the future strategies and plans of SCLC.

* The FBI continues to discredit the dead King even in 2020.

Demonstrations in St Augustine

Founded in 1565 by Spanish colonisers, this oldest city of America (settled by Europeans) was almost totally segregated. In a wise, tactical move, King chose St Augustine as the center of his next campaign. It was gripped by a celebratory fervour, as it was about to celebrate its four hundredth birthday and was hopeful of receiving federal financial assistance.

This city was a haven for the violent activities of the Ku Klux Klan, which had time and again indulged in intimidatory tactics, even scaring and threatening those white businessmen who tried to desegregate their shops.

Dr RN Hayling, a black dentist of St Augustine, and head of the local NAACP had courageously fought segregation here since 1959 but to no avail. In June 1963, he organised the Youth Council of the local chapter of NAACP, which began protests in front of Woolworths on King Street, fronting the plaza. They demonstrated, carrying placards which said, '*If we spend money here, why can't we eat?*'

Although the total population of fifteen thousand comprised twenty-five per cent blacks, yet they had no civil liberties. In September 1963, Dr Hayling and three other black activists – Clyde Jenkins, James Jackson, and James Houser – were kidnapped by Klansmen and almost suffered a fiery annihilation. In February 1964 when Dr Hayling resigned his NAACP office, his house was dynamited; his wife and children narrowly missed being killed.

Instances of violence gained momentum day by day. In early February 1964, the houses of two black families whose children had integrated public schools were also set on fire;

the authorities regarded the violence committed against the blacks with a heartless apathy. Sheriff LO Davies, a vocal segregationist, went to the length of organising a force of hundred volunteers, most of them known Klansmen headed by Holsted 'Hoss' Manucy, who went about terrorising the blacks.

The brutalised blacks were left to their own resources, as Hoss Manucy venomously proclaimed, 'my boys are here to fight niggers', and Manucy's Raiders, as the townspeople called them, made nocturnal assaults on the blacks.

When King came to St Augustine, Hoss Manucy scornfully poured venom at him, calling him an 'outside nigger', and that he wouldn't have anything to do with outsiders.

Racial injustices were being perpetrated in St Augustine regarding which Andrew Young of the SCLC proclaimed, 'When you have one man, wearing civilian clothes, beating you, while another, wearing a badge standing, waiting to arrest you when the first gets tired, well, that makes you think, St Augustine is really worse than Birmingham. It's the worst I've ever seen.'

While the cauldron of racial injustice bubbled in St Augustine, few people outside paid any heed to it, but something happened on 29 March 1964, as a result of which all eyes were riveted on this racial cauldron. On that day Easter Sunday, nine members of an interracial group of women refused to leave the dining room of the 'Whites Only' Monson Motor court, with the result that they were arrested. Among those were 72-year old Mrs Malcolm Peabody, mother of the Governor of Massachusetts, Endcott Peabody, and the wife of the first black Episcopal Bishop, Mrs John Burgess, who were arrested when they led a sit-in at the Ponce De Leon Restaurant.

This made front-page news on 1 April 1964.

The pathetic condition of the blacks and the unjust segregation rampant in St Augustine made national headlines, and the grievances of the blacks gained national publicity.

In the meantime, Dr Hayling, who had become the head of the St Augustine SCLC, had started feeling the absolute necessity of King's presence in St Augustine, otherwise he was afraid the movement would fail. Accordingly, in March 1964, Dr Hayling, Henry and Catherine Twine, and other leaders asked King and SCLC to intervene in April 1964. Afraid that the proposed Civil Rights Bill being filibustered in the US senate would be defeated, King and other leaders hastened to St Augustine to make a stand, also rallying the support of Northern supporters.

Demonstrators were driven into the water by segregationists when they tried to integrate the beaches of Anastasia Island, and some nearly drowned. They were kept in a stockade during the day under the relentless fury of the sun, as the jails were overcrowded.

In May 1964, Hosea Williams [Director, SCLC field staff, 1963 - 1970] decided to dramatise the pathetic condition of the black population by starting nocturnal marches to the slave market. This market, which symbolised oppression and injustice, was ironically situated in the city's Constitution Plaza. King also approved of such marches as an instrument of arousing the 'creative tension' essential for highlighting the racial violence in St Augustine; thus, coercing the federal government into defending the Civil Rights of black Americans.

Niggers ain't Got no God

Hosea Williams and Dr Hayling launched a recruitment drive, recruiting school and college students, trained them in non-violence, and prepared them for the night marches. On Tuesday, 26 May 1964, an army of about four-hundred non-violent marchers, led by Andrew Young, left the First Baptist Church at night, and headed towards the slave market. This was also the night of the Florida gubernatorial race. As the disciplined army of peaceful marchers marched past the campaign headquarters of Haydon Burns, a segregationist candidate, there was a threatening cry from one of the bystanders: 'If our man's in, you niggers have had it.' Their man, Haydon, was in.

The following night, about hundred Klansmen armed with iron pipes and chains, screaming '*Niggers ain't got no God*', waited at the slave market to carry out their threat as five-hundred marchers led by Young left St Mary's Baptist Church and arrived at the slave market. But this time, the marchers merely circled the Plaza and reached the Church, unmolested. On the evening of Thursday, 28 May 1964, another group left St Paul's AME Church, headed by Young. No sooner had they reached the slave market, than they were assaulted by Klansmen, carrying iron pipes and chains. As they dropped to their knees to pray, one of the Klansmen yelled: '*Niggers ain't got no God!*'

While the police twiddled their thumbs, and looked the other way, the non-violent marchers were brutalised and battered in the presence of television cameras and reporters.

The following day, King telegraphed President Johnson, appealing for federal intervention, reiterating that they could not postpone the non-violent thrust merely because violence had erupted, but sincerely believed that, as American citizens, their right to peaceful assembly must be guaranteed and not abridged because of the unrestrained lawlessness of the Klan element.

His plea for federal intervention was turned down by the Johnson administration and, the black citizens of St Augustine were indignant when the federal government granted the city's request for $350,000 to help finance its quadri-centennial celebrations.

The night marches were banned in St Augustine by a local court injunction on 31 May. Tension escalated and the same day, King arrived along with some press members. He issued a plea to '*all men of conscience*' to join him in the forthcoming demonstrations. By obtaining the court order, Sheriff Davis had inadvertently helped their cause. On 1 June 1964, King along with SCLC lawyers requested Judge Bryan Simpson of the US District Court in Jacksonville to reverse the injunction, as it violated the First Amendment rights of the protestors to freedom of speech and assembly.

While waiting for the verdict, King tried to inculcate the virtues of non-violence in the blacks. Then came good news from Jacksonville on 9 June 1964, Judge Simpson, ruling in favour of King and SCLC, declared that there will be no further interference with the night marches. He also exposed the connivance of the police department in the Klan atrocities.

However, a federal court ruling did not deter the white segregationists from indulging in violence and intimidatory tactics. An undaunted King declared: '*We are determined (that) this city will not celebrate its quadri-centennial as a segregated city. There will be no turning back.*'

On 10 June 1964, the Senate filibuster against the Civil Rights Bill was finally defeated in a 71 to 29 vote. The Senate had voted to close off debate on a Civil Rights filibuster for the first time in history. The passage of the Bill could not be stopped now.

On Thursday, 11 June 1964, King was arrested on the steps of the Monson motel restaurant along with Ralph Abernathy and some others when they tried to integrate the restaurant for violating Florida's unwanted guest law. What followed was another letter, this time '*a letter from the St Augustine Jail*', to his old friend Rabbi Israel Dresner in New Jersey asking him to recruit rabbis to take part in the movement in St Augustine. This was followed by the largest mass arrest of rabbis in America on 18 June 1964 at Monson Hotel Lodge.

The climactic moment of the demonstrations came when some protestors jumped into the swimming pool at the Monson

Motor Lodge on 18 June 1964 and James Brock, the President of the Florida Hotel and Motel Association, tried to pour acid into the pool to get the demonstrators out. The photographs of these atrocities were emblazoned on the world conscience, which was horrified at this brutal outrage. The same evening, some four-hundred demonstrators were attacked by white mobsters near the slave market, there being some semblance of order only with the arrival of the state troopers who set off tear gas bombs.

On 12 June 1964, JB Stoner, an Atlanta attorney spewed venom and racial hatred in an effort to arouse racist sentiment: 'When the constitution said, all men are created equal, it wasn't talking about niggers. The coons have been parading around St Augustine for a long time.' This irate mob of white segregationists later headed towards the black section of the town. They carried confederate flags and signs: 'KILL THE CIVIL RIGHTS BILL and PUT GEORGE WALLACE ON THE SUPREME COURT.'

One hundred-and-seventy white marchers suffused with racial hatred and accompanied by ferocious police dogs and state troopers arrived at the black neighbourhood only to be greeted by the sign: 'WELCOME, PEACE AND BROTHERHOOD TO YOU.'

Violence was face-to-face with non-violence. King's non-violent disciples had steadfastly refused to meet violence with violence.

King gets Honorary Degree from Yale University

Hopeful of a victory for the Civil Rights Bill, King flew directly to Yale University to receive an honorary degree, after being released from jail on 14 June 1964, on a $900 bail.

There was a deafening applause from ten thousand spectators, as Yale President, Kingman Brewster, commended the remarkable leader of men for having kindled the nation's sense of outrage at the injustices inflicted upon black Americans, and for his steadfast refusal to counter violence with violence.

Meanwhile, violence continued unabated in St Augustine, making King remark that it was '*the most lawless community he had ever seen*'. Constant pressure was needed to be applied on the white power structure, so despite the recommendations of the Grand Jury, appointed on 11 June 1964 to stop all demonstrations for 30 days, and their insistence that King and the SCLC leave St Augustine for 30 days, King outrightly rejected such a proposal. He offered a counter proposal for a one week moratorium on protests, and an immediate establishment of a bi-racial committee.

On 25 June 1964, black demonstrators were again brazenly assaulted at the slave market by eight hundred Klansmen led by Hoss Manuci. A *Newsweek* reporter, who tried to intervene to protect a thirteen-year old black girl from being mauled, was also severely thrashed.

The next day, at the risk of facing contempt of court charges, night marches were banned by Governor Farris Bryant and, on 30 June 1964, he announced the creation of an emergency bi-racial committee of four unnamed men to 'restore communication' between the white and black communities. King hailed it as '*a creative and important first step*,' he suspended demonstrations on 30 June 1964, and closing down his headquarters, departed for Atlanta with SCLC on 1 July 1964.

Earlier, in anticipation of the passage of the Civil Rights Bill, nearly eighty hotels of the city had agreed to desegregate their facilities, and King hoped that the passage of the Bill would do the rest.

The passage of the Civil Rights Bill

After eighty-three days of debate, a historical day dawned for the black freedom movement. The US Senate passed the Civil Rights Bill on 19 June 1964 by a vote of 73 to 27 and returned it to the House for final approval. This was followed by a mixed reaction. King hailed it as *'a lasting tribute to the memory of John F Kennedy'*. For others, like Senator Strom Thurmond, it was a sad day for America.

On 2 July 1964, President Johnson signed the Bill into law. 'The new law', said President Johnson, *'does not give special treatment to any citizen. It does, however, say that "those who are equal before God shall now also be equal in the polling booths, in the classrooms, in the factories and in hotels and restaurants and movie theatres, and other places that provide service to the public."'*

'It was an act of good faith,' King proclaimed.

Although the Civil Rights Act was another milestone in the black freedom struggle, and although it was stronger than the original proposal of Kennedy, yet, it was not altogether satisfactory. It lacked a strong voting rights clause.

President Lyndon Johnson shakes hands with the Martin Luther King Jr after handing him one of the pens used in signing the Civil Rights Act of 2 July 1964 at the White House in Washington

Courtesy: American Centre, New Delhi

SELMA AND THE VOTING RIGHTS ACT 1965

NO WAVE of racism could stop them, no mighty armies could intimidate them. Undeterred by ferocious dogs and lynching, nocturnal assaults and pressure tactics, the blacks were bracing themselves for storming more bastions. They were getting ready for another season of suffering, another non-violent battle, another dramatic confrontation with the racist order.

This time they chose the City of Selma, Alabama, as their non-violent battlefield, where the voting conditions were pathetic. In 1965, there were about 13,000 whites and 14,500 blacks in Selma, and less than two per cent of them were registered to vote. Since 1963, the SNCC had been actively trying to arouse local blacks and lead voter registration drives, but to no avail.

When the SCLC decided to focus its attention on Selma, there was a lot of resentment in the SNCC because they felt they had already done the ground work in Selma and were apprehensive that the SCLC would finally take the credit, if the movement was successful.

On 2 January 1965, King arrived in Selma, and

addressing a crowd of about 700 people at Brown's Chapel African Methodist Episcopal Church, said that they had chosen Selma as their battlefield this time because of the fact that it had become a symbol of bitter-end resistance to the Civil Rights movement in the deep South. He proclaimed: '*We are going to start a march on the ballot boxes by the thousands … we must be willing to go to jail by the thousands. We are not asking, we are demanding the ballot.*'

After initial apprehensions, the SNCC also threw in its lot with the SCLC, and they started almost daily marches to the county courthouse in downtown Selma, within Sheriff Jim Clark's jurisdiction. They were determined to have the ballot and '*determined to have it now so that they could become the masters of their own destinies*'.

Black suffrage had been a major goal for King since 1957, when he led the Prayer Pilgrimage to Washington to demand the ballot. He hailed this campaign as the most powerful and dramatic Civil Rights protest that had ever taken place in the South.

On 18 January 1965, after he returned to Selma from the west coast, where he had addressed many religious and civic groups to garner support, King became the first black man to register at the century-old Albert Hotel. Here he was assaulted by a white man who was then arrested soon after.

They desperately needed a crisis by provoking Sheriff Jim Clark into his characteristic brutality. They were also on the lookout for an incident that would get them national attention which they got on Tuesday, 19 January 1965 when Amelia Boynton, a Civil Rights activist, was grabbed by the collar by Sheriff Clark and pushed for half a block into a police car. King described it as '*one of the most brutal and unlawful acts*' he had ever seen an officer commit.

The next morning, photographs of this brutality were splashed all over many newspapers, including *The New York Times* and *The Washington Post.* This was followed by successive marches in which many blacks were arrested.

On Monday, 25 January 1965, a fifty-three-year-old activist, Annie Lee Cooper, was clubbed on her head by Sheriff Clark. The nation's sensibilities were again hurt when photographs of this incident made to the national press.

On 1 February 1965, King and Ralph Abernathy were arrested along with others for parading without a permit when they lead a united group of 15 whites and 250 blacks from Brown's Chapel to the Selma court house. The others were released on bail the same day, but King and Abernathy preferred to remain in prison for five days, aware of the publicity that it would fetch their cause. From his jail cell, King wrote, '*This is Selma, Alabama. There are more Negroes in jail with me than there are on the voting rolls.*'

On 5 February 1965, King's short letter from Selma jail appeared as an advertisement in *The New York Times.*

On 18 February 1965, a twenty-six-year-old black demonstrator, Jimmie Lee Jackson, was fatally shot by state troopers during a demonstration in Marion, Alabama, thirty miles from Selma. A surge of indignation swept across the SCLC; it decided to march from Selma to Montgomery for protesting against the killing and to submit a petition to Governor Wallace to enforce black voting rights.

By this time, the relations between SNCC and SCLC had reached a stage when they did not see eye to eye on many issues. The idea of the march did not appeal to many SNCC members. As chairman of the SNCC, John Lewis, however, maintained that '*the people of Alabama wanted to march; they had a right to march, and I was going to go and march with them*'. So, it was agreed that the SNCC members could participate in the march on an individual basis.

The Selma March comprised three marches:

Bloody Sunday: 7 March 1965

The first march look place on 7 March 1965, during which demonstrators were beaten up, as they tried to cross Edmund Pettus Bridge. The brutalities unleashed by Sheriff Clark's men spread around the world in no time, and the *Bloody Sunday*, as the newspapers called this day, horrified all right-thinking people. Shocked at this violence, King vowed to lead another march.

Turnaround Tuesday: 9 March 1965

Although the federal court issued a temporary injunction against the upcoming march, King declared that he would '*die on the highway than make a butchery of his conscience*'. He truncated the march halfway to Montgomery, asking his men to turn around, and go back across Edmund Pettus Bridge into Selma; that way he would not be violating the federal injunction. Some criticised King for this move, calling it a 'betrayal'. Others like Burke Marshall, the former Head of the Justice Department's Civil Rights Division, later conceded that King showed '*tremendous courage in walking the line between the two contending forces, making his protest without having defied the federal courts.*'

Death of James Reeb: 11 March 1965

Meanwhile, the viciousness of racism shocked the world once again when a white Unitarian Minister, James Reeb (1 January 1927 – 11 March 1965), who had worked in the black ghetto in Boston and who had also bought a house in the Negro section, and had come to support King after *Bloody Sunday*, being one of the dozen white UU (Unitarian Universalist) Ministers to have done so, was murderously assaulted on 9 March 1965.

Soon after the march on 9 March 1965, on his very first night in Selma, a group of white racists attacked him and two more clergymen, Rev Orloff Miller and Rev Clark Olsen, with iron pipes, as they left a black-owned restaurant, *Eddie's Place*, in Selma after having dinner, at 7:30 pm. He succumbed to his injuries two days later.

In the ecumenical service, King exhorted the congregated men and women to leave the ivory towers of learning and storm the bastions of segregation and see to it that the work Jim Reeb had started, be continued so that the white south might come to terms with its conscience.

While eulogising Rev Reeb, King quoted from Shakespeare's *Romeo and Juliet.*

And if he should die,
Take his body, and cut it into little stars.
He will make the face of heaven so fine.
That all the world will be in love with night.

King's speech was followed by the appearance of a new figure at the microphone who made the thrilling announcement that the federal court had upheld their right to march to the Dallas County Courthouse and hold a service there.

Although two weeks earlier, Jimmy Lee Jackson had also been killed, the national outcry that followed Rev James Reeb's brutal murder was instrumental in quickening the passage of the federal Voting Rights Act. The same evening, on 15 March 1965, President Johnson presented a Bill to the joint session of Congress, which would later become the Voting Right Act.

Speaking in front of the Congress, President Johnson said:

> Even if we pass this bill, the battle will not be over, what happened in Selma is part of a far longer movement which reaches into every section and state of America. It is the effort of American Negroes to secure for themselves the full blessings of American life. Their cause must be our cause too, because it is not just Negroes but really it is all of us who must overcome the crippling legacy of bigotry and injustice. And we shall overcome.

The use of '*we shall overcome*' by President Johnson was a cathartic moment for King and the other Civil Rights activists.

'I looked over…and Martin was very quietly sitting in the chair, and a tear ran down his cheek. It was a victory like none other. It was an affirmation of the movement,' said CT Vivian, a Civil Rights activist, who was with King when the speech was broadcast.

On 15 March 1965, a federal court had overruled the City of Selma's ban on demonstrations, and this thoughtful decision by a US district Judge, Frank Johnson, implied that the blacks now had a legal and constitutional right to march from Selma

Selma to Motgomery Civil Rights March, 1965

to Montgomery and, accordingly, for the next few days, the eyes of the world were upon America as the march started once again with full vigour.

On 16 March 1965, James Forman led a group of about 600 students in a protest at the Montgomery County Courthouse, where the protestors were attacked by Police on horseback. Apprehensive of violence, King also hastened to Montgomery. Addressing a group of about a thousand people, Forman called for a massive direct action in Montgomery that would '*tie up every street and bus, and commit every act of civil disobedience ever seen*'.

On 17 March 1965, King told the demonstrators, '*We are here to say to the white man that we will no longer let them use their clubs on us in the dark corners. We're going to make them do it in the glaring light of television.*'

THE DEATH OF VIOLA LIUZZO

ON THE final night of the march, on 25 March 1965, the triumph and jubilation of the previous hours was cruelly shattered, when a white volunteer, Viola Liuzzo, from Detroit, after having driven one carload to Selma, was shot dead by Klansmen, when on her way back to Montgomery with her nineteen-year-old black guide, Leroy Moton, to pick up another group. A car, with four Klansmen, ambushed them, shooting Viola on her head and killing her; the car fell in a ditch, Moton survived by feigning death.

Viola Liuzzo (11 April 1925 – 25 March 1965), a thirty-nine-year-old mother of five, and a Universalist Civil Rights activist, having arrived in Selma six days earlier in response to King's call to add her voice to the cry for justice, had died for a sacred battle, the rights of humanity, as her husband, Anthony Liuzzo, put it. President Johnson consoled him, 'I don'*t think she died in vain because this was going to be a battle, all out, as far as I'm concerned ...*'

Within twenty-four hours, President Johnson condemned this cowardly murder on nationwide television, announcing Mrs Liuzzo had been '*murdered by the enemies of justice, who for decades have used the rape and the gun, the tar and the feathers to terrorise their neighbours. They struck by night... for their purpose cannot stand the light of day*'.

Passage of the Voting Rights Act

Another historical day dawned on 6 August 1965, when '*the most powerful and dramatic civil rights protest*' that had ever taken place in the South culminated in the passage of the new Voting Rights Act. This law opened the voting booth to two-and-a-half million previously disenfranchised Southern blacks, empowering the Attorney General to send federal registrars into any county where there were instances of discrimination. Poll taxes, literacy tests, and other prerequisites which had been used to disqualify black voters were abolished.

Selma had successfully dramatised the indignities and injustices that the Negroes had suffered in the South, situations had cried for intervention, and the crisis-provoking strategy of King and SCLC had again coerced the federal government to respond to mounting national indignation by enforcing Civil Rights in the deep south.

President Johnson called the legislation '*one of the most monumental laws in the entire history of American freedom*' and John Lewis said: '*This milestone was every bit as momentous, and significant... as the emancipation proclamation or the 1954 Supreme Court decision*'.

Before leaving Brown Chapel on the five-day march from Selma to Montgomery, King had spoken to the marchers: '*We are on the move now. Like an idea whose time has come, not even the marching of mighty armies can halt us. We're moving to the land of freedom.*'

They had finally moved to the '*land of freedom*'; no wave of racism had stopped them. Their time appeared to have come.

[Forty-four years after the Selma March, many remembered the days of the march, when they either turned up for President Barack Obama's inauguration ceremony in January 2009, or watched it on television.]

An eighteen-year old youth, Bobby Simmons, did something during the Selma Voting Rights Campaign that became symbolic of the campaign. He wrote *VOTE* across his forehead with sunscreen, and was clicked by a photographer.

[Sixty-two years old, at the time of President Barack Obama's inauguration, Simmons was not present in Washington but watched the ceremony from his home in Selma. For him, it was a '*dream of a lifetime*' after having undergone a lot of disillusionment, deprivation and discrimination, the dream had finally been realised.]

Sister Roberta Schmidt, a white nun, was among the first group of people from all faiths and backgrounds to show up in Selma for a march to the Courthouse before they were stopped by the police. This member of the Sisters of St Joseph of Carondelet in St Louis had hastened to Selma in response to King's plea for help.

[This educator, who lived in Venice during the inauguration ceremony of Barack Obama, hoped that the 'excitement over the president elect will call attention to humankind.'

In the graduation ceremony of Avila University on 9 May 2015, she was felicitated with Honorary Doctorate of Human Letters along with two more sisters, Rosemary Flanigan and Barbara Moore, all Avila alumnae, who were part of the iconic Selma march.]

'*We all predicted that this would happen one day. But Barack's election is not the utopia we dreamed about. We are still in the process of getting there. We are better off than we were 50 years ago, but there is still discrimination and segregation in America*,' thus spoke Juanita Abernathy (77), wife of Rev Ralph Abernathy, Martin's close friend and confidante, who along with many others had marched on, unafraid on the front lines of the movement.

A WAR ON POVERTY PROGRAMME

A WAR on Poverty Programme was launched by President Johnson after his landslide victory in the Presidential election in 1964. In his Annual Message to the Congress on the State of the Union on 8 Jan 1964, Johnson declared:

> Let this session of Congress be known as the session which did more for Civil Rights than the last hundred sessions combined ... as the session which declared all-out war on human poverty and unemployment.
>
> Unfortunately, many Americans live on the outskirts of hope, some because of their poverty, and some because of their colour, and all too many because of both. Our task is to help replace their despair with opportunity.

Thus, President Johnson refusing to '*fritter and fumble away our opportunities in needless, senseless quarrels*', declared an unconditional war on poverty in America, emphasising '*better schools and better health and better homes, and better training and better job opportunities*'. The programme was announced when the poverty level had fallen from 22.4 per cent in 1959 to 19 per cent in 1964.

On 15 March 1965, in a nationally televised address to Congress, President Johnson conceded that the conditions of impoverished Americans could be improved not merely through equal opportunity, but it was important that the nation should give all our people – Black and White – the help that they need to walk through those gates.

This Johnsonian acknowledgement was followed by another historic commencement address at Howard University in Washington DC on 4 June 1965, wherein Johnson argued that, in order to compensate the blacks for generations of inherited disadvantages, they must be granted preferential treatment. Emphasising factual equality and not merely theoretical equality, he concluded that the '*next and more profound stage of the battle of Civil Rights was to discover ways in which blacks might move beyond opportunity to achievement*'. In order to fulfill there rights, Johnson announced that he would invite black leaders, experts, scholars and government officials for a White House Conference.

The Civil Rights leaders received the Howard University speech with a lot of optimism, hoping that the federal government would now try to promote full equality for black Americans. One reporter remarked '*not since Lincoln signed the Emancipation Proclamation had Negroes been offered such hope*'.

In the concluding chapter of *Why We Can't Wait* (1964), King put forth the argument that the black American's freedom could be meaningfully substantial only when equal opportunity was combined with '*the practical realistic aid which will help him to seize it*'. Responding to Johnson's war on poverty, he emphasised '*a broad-based and gigantic Bill of Rights for the disadvantaged'*. He maintained that just as the state compensated World War II veterans for the time they spent away from their jobs and homes, it should also compensate blacks for their years of enslavement.

Although, the Civil Rights movement had won quite a few victories, the American Dilemma was still as unresolved as ever. In fact, some discordant notes were struck by many white Americans who were not quite happy with the strides made by the black Americans, believing that the Johnson administration was being too speedy with racial integration.

The ghettos of the North were characterised by pathetic living conditions where the Civil Rights Act of 1964 and the Voting Rights Act of 1965 had done little to transform the deplorable living conditions. Police brutality, unemployment, poverty, de-facto segregation were very much in vogue here and a major portion of black Americans did not have the economic wherewithal to make more strides in socio-economic fields. At the meeting of the platform committee of the Republican National Convention in San Fransisco, on 7 July 1965, King claimed that few people consider the fact that, in addition to being enslaved for two centuries, '*the Negro was, during all those years, robbed of the wages of his toil*'. He firmly believed that nothing could provide adequate compensation for the psychological havoc resulting from centuries of servitude.

Later, at the platform committee of the democratic National convention in Atlanta city in August 1964, he further emphasised the same part and argued for a full programme of free quality education and learning plus broad health services.

In his best-seller, *The Fire Next Time* (1963) James Baldwin had made a sinister prophecy implying that black Americans '*may never be able to rise to power, but they are very well-placed indeed to precipitate chaos and ring down the curtain on the American Dream*'.

This prophecy appeared to ring dangerously true when Watts, the black ghetto of Los Angels, broke out in violence in August 1965. This was the most severe race riot in the country's history, leaving destruction to the tune of four million USDs in its wake, besides 1,032 injured and 34 dead.

King had cited five major areas that the proposed anti-poverty bill would address: employment, education, health and welfare, housing and the rural poor. It was precisely the lack of these necessities that found expression in the gruesome violence in Watts.

Marquette Frye, a twenty-one-year-old black man was arrested for drunk driving on the border of Los Angeles, Watts neighbourhood on a suffocating hot evening Wednesday, 11 August 1965, which sparked off rioting for six days, wherein looting was all-pervasive. Riots intensified by Friday and by Saturday night, a curfew was imposed, and almost 14,000 National Guard troops patrolled a 45-mile area.

Afraid that the ghetto residents would be pushed further into despair and hopelessness, King arrived in Watts on Tuesday, 17 August 1965, after having cut short his stay in Puerto Rico. But by the time he arrived, the curfew had been lifted, and the riots were mostly over. On his arrival, he argued that the problems that led to the violence in Watt were environmental and not racial; the economic deprivation, social violation, inadequate housing and the general despair of thousands of Negroes teeming in the Northern and Western ghettos are the ready seeds, which give birth to tragic expression of violence.

Offering to mediate between the local people and the government officials, and trying to bridge the rift between blacks and whites, he looked for solutions to the socio-economic problems with which Watts and other black ghettos were besieged.

Talking to reporters on 20 August 1965, King argued that the Watts riots were the beginning of a stirring of those people in the society who have been passed by the progress of the past decade. He also maintained that, in the North, the struggles were about '*dignity and work*' while in the South, they were about '*rights*'.

While interacting with local people, he was alarmed by

their strong belief that they could make people listen to them only through an armed insurrection. He talked to President Johnson immediately and suggested a federal anti-poverty programme in Los Angeles, which President Johnson agreed, and praised him for '*doing a good job going out there*'.

After SCLC launched its Chicago Campaign, King lamented the destruction that had followed in the wake of the riots. He asked an audience in Chicago, '*What did Watts accomplish but the death of 34 Negroes and injury to thousands more? What did it profit the Negro to burn down the stores and factories in which he sought employment? The way of riots is not a way of progress, but a blind ally of death and destruction, which wrecks its havoc hardest against the rioters themselves.*'

Shortly after the Watts riot, King wrote an article in the *Saturday Review: "Next Stop: The North"*, in which he maintained that 'urban poverty' should be the issue that should now be tackled by the movement. It was the simmering discontent in Watts that had found expression in the blood-curdling violence, and unless positive steps were taken to improve the condition of the ghettos, the Watts violence could be repeated elsewhere. He observed '*the cohesive, potentially explosive Negro community in the North has a short fuse and a long train of abuses*'.

Holding a plea for nonviolence, he reiterated that the North could also be transformed as the South had been, if non-violence could be employed on a mass scale. He said, '*If one hundred thousand Negroes march in a major city to a strategic location, they will make municipal operations difficult to conduct, they will exceed the capacity of even the most reckless mayor to use force against them.*'

The Chicago Movement

In order to reinvigorate and energise the black freedom struggle, King had often visited Chicago during the first decade of his public career. But in 1966, King and SCLC arrived there on a different – mission to kick off a non-violent protest campaign, its first sustained Northern movement. It marked a significant transition in his life and the life of the SCLC.

Three years prior to SCLC arrival in Chicago, a coalition of thirty-four Civil Rights, religious and civil groups – Coordinating Council of Community Organisations (CCCO) – headed by Albert Raby, had been tirelessly protesting against de-facto segregation in Chicago public schools through non-violent means. On a brief visit to Chicago to boost Raby's campaign, King led a march of about three thousand demonstrators to City Hall on 26 July 1965, delivering speeches and touring the city's ghettos, receiving a lot of publicity.

Ruthless racial lines were drawn here and it was sometimes called the nation's '*most segregated*' city. This great mid-western metropolis – the largest city in the United States – was home to some of the worst ghetto problems. The city had a total population of about three and a half million, out of which almost one million were black, and a greater number resided in slums on the South and Westside.

It was into one such slum that King, in a highly symbolic move, shifted his family, on 26 January 1966, to a rented apartment located at 1550, South Hamlin Avenue on the west side of the city of Chicago, North Lawndale, where he hoped to live three days a week. The rest of his time would be spent at the SCLC headquarters in Atlanta, or in touring cities, trying to raise money for the Chicago movement. On James Bevel's shoulders fell the responsibility of the day-to- day supervision of the campaign. The campaign headquarters were established at the *Warren Avenue Congregational Church*, located on Chicago's west side in the East Garfield Section.

A population of about three hundred thousand blacks was packed in its 800 square blocks, many of them having come from the South to escape the Jim Crow Laws. '*You can't really get close to the poor without living and being with them*,' King told the reporters gathered there. In an effort to show his sympathy for the poor, he shifted to this third floor four-room aging apartment, which the local press labelled a publicity stunt but some hoped for positive results.

It was the neighborhood's poverty that induced King to choose North Lawndale as his base for the Northern Civil Rights movement. Besides poverty, all poverty-related problems were rampant here – unemployment, crime, poor housing, and corruption. King wanted to draw the attention of the government to the poor housing conditions here. James Bevel labeled the Lawndale area as *Slumdale.* King defined a slum as '*little more than a domestic colony, which leaves its inhabitants dominated politically, exploited economically, (and) segregated and humiliated at every time.*'

In these slums, all this was prevalent and some felt that his presence might draw swift action. King himself felt that his arrival raised local morale, as he walked the neighborhood, visited a school, and even shot pool in a neighborhood drive.

Chicago Sun-Times sardonically remarked that if he merely kept moving he might single-handedly clean up the city's slums.

THE JAMES MEREDITH MARCH ON FEAR

WHILE ATTENDING Jackson State College (1960-62), James Meredith had tried to gain admission to the University of Mississippi. After his application was rejected in 1961, he filed a complaint with the District Court on 31 May 1961, alleging that he had been denied admission because of his race. The District Court rejected these allegations. However, on appeal, the fifth Judicial Circuit Court reversed this ruling, maintaining that Mississippi was indeed maintaining a policy of educational segregation.

This decision was violently opposed by the students and state officials. In spite of the constant fear of being lynched, Meredeth was able to graduate in 1964.

On 5 June 1966, Meredith and four of his friends set off on foot from Memphsis, Tennessee, to protest against racism. He wanted to show to the world that blacks could no longer be threatened and intimidated.

On 6 June 1966, while on a 220-mile pilgrimage along Highway 51, when he was hardly ten miles away from his home state of Mississippi, he was blasted in the back with a shotgun. Not wanting to be taken to a Mississippi hospital, he was taken back to a Memphsis hospital, where King and other Civil Rights leaders rushed to him and, through mutual consent, decided that the march should not stop. Meredith remarked, '*Yes, this thing is bigger than any individual. It's bigger than me.*'

King believed that, before they arrived safely in the Promised Land, '*there were still prodigious hilltops of opposition and gigantic mountains of injustice and resistance*' to be conquered. These hilltops of opposition, they met in the form of those young people from the CORE and the SNCC, who proclaimed the efficacy of Black Power, and started doubting the relevance of the non-violent approach.

There was an acrimonious debate among the leaders; some like 24-year-old Stokley Carmichael, who had only recently reelected John Lewis as the chairman of the SNCC, advocating an all-black march and some, like Roy Wilkins of the NAACP, who supported integration and believed that the white liberals could not be alienated from their movement. Finally yielding to King's passionate and sincere eloquence, the detractors decided to follow the path of non-violence, and even agreed to welcome white liberals on the march.

The James Meredith March against Fear covered two hundred miles and lasted three weeks, during which the movement teetered on the brink of a precarious split, nonviolence being pitted against violence. On 8 June 1966, Floyd McKessick, King and Stokley Carmichael resumed the march from the place where Meredith had been wounded, under police protection.

A new slogan was raised during the march by Stokley Carmichael – *Black Power*. While the *CORE* voted to adopt this slogan, the NAACP denounced it. The younger and more radical leaders failed to see eye-to-eye with King's philosophy of non-violence, which caused him intense pain.

King could sense resentment amongst some black activists against the invasion of the white activists in their movement; while singing the Civil Rights anthem '*we shall overcome*', some blacks became silent at the words '*black and white together*'. Some suggested that they should not sing '*we shall overcome*' but '*we shall overrun*'. King reiterated, '*I'm tired of violence ... and I'm not going to let my oppressor dictate to me what method I must use... we have a power... a power that cannot be found in bullets and guns.*'

The movement got sadly fragmented around two opposing rallying cries – '*Black Power*' and '*Freedom Now*', which King and the SCLC upheld. To King, *Black Power* was synonymous with violence, and he believed that, as a slogan, it was counterproductive.

King suffered some of the most dangerous and heart-wrenching moments of his life during this march, the constant fear of being attacked always hovered in the background, apart from the denunciation of his philosophy of non-violence. Floyd McKissick emphasised the uselessness of non-violence in racist America.

They tried to register black voters while marching through Mississippi. In Grenada, they lead 13,00 prospective voters to the Courthouse. They were shocked to find that there was hardly any positive change in Grenada since the Civil War.

Restrooms and water fountains at the Courthouse were still out of bounds for the blacks.

Martin Luther King Jr with Joan Baez

With a fierce defiant determination, they drank from the water fountains and used the restrooms ushering in some change after hundred years.

King's two older children joined King for the final leg of the Mississippi march.

In Greenwood, Stokley Carmichael declared, 'We're asking Negroes not to go to Vietnam and fight, but to stay in Greenwood, and fight here.' He was arrested for attempting to erect a tent on the grounds of a black school. Speaking to a huge rally after his release he said, 'This is the twenty-seventh time I have been arrested, and I ain't going to jail no more.'

This was the trial period of King's philosophy of non-violence. Young Stokley Carmichael and his ideology of *Black Power*, with all its volatile aspects, was now hitting the newspaper headlines filling King, and the other proponents of non-violence, with misgivings. So, he called a meeting at a small Catholic Parish house in Yazoo city, Mississippi, where he maintained that so far as *Black Power* implied self-determination for black Americans – by consolidation of their political and economic resources – he had nothing against it, but its violent connotations could be suicidal for the movement. Carmichael's argument that blacks could progress only by attainment of economic and political power was met by a counter argument by King that the Italian, Irish and Jewish immigrants had attained such power in America through creative endeavour and group unity, not through a slogan.

The Yazoo conference concluded after five hours of heated debate. It was agreed that neither '*Black Power*' nor '*Freedom Now*' would be used for the rest of the pilgrimage to Jackson. But the slogan '*Black Power*' had caught on and to King's utter disgust, certain sections of the people continued to find it appealing. The hate-filled rhetoric emanating from such an ideology fell on his ears like '*strange music from a foreign land*'. As he said later, '*My hearing was not attuned to the sound of such bitterness.*'

The march, however, remained peaceful, until the group decided to make a detour to Philadelphia, Mississippi, during the final week of the Freedom March. Two years earlier, three Civil Rights activists – James Chaney, Andrew Goodman and Michael Schwerner – had been killed, and King intended to hold a memorial service for these martyrs at the local Courthouse.

On the arrival of King and his group of about 250 marchers, they were attacked by irate whites with clubs. Sheriff Lawrence Rainey and Chief Deputy Cecil Price – both under indictment for the murder of the three – stood by and watched, while taunts and cherry bombs were hurled during King's speech. The marchers were again attacked during the night when they tried to sleep at their campsite. King vowed to return to Philadelphia after a few days; he wired the President seeking police protection but there was no response.

About 2,000 marchers arrived in Canton, Mississippi, on 23 June 1966, where they were again attacked when, in defiance of an order, they pitched tents on the grounds of a black elementary school. The violence that ensued was sadly reminiscent of 'Bloody Sunday' in Selma a year ago. As President Johnson's silence was unnerving, such administrative snubs made the *Black Power* slogan appear tantalising.

King returned to Philadelphia on 24 June 1966, accompanied by some 300 non-violent marchers and in defiance of Sheriff Rainey's order, forbidding them to climb the Courthouse steps to pray, he knelt with Ralph Abernathy on the Courthouse steps to pray, and then led the marchers out of Philadelphia and back to the route the march had taken.

Abernathy later recalled: '*It was one of the most fearful experiences we had in the movement period, and even King admitted that I just knew I'd never see (the end of) the day.*' But they stuck together and worked together in their most fearful moments.

On 27 June 1966, a scorching Sunday, the marchers arrived at the state capital in Jackson, after spending three weeks on the road.

To the accompaniment of a band, which played '*when the saints go marching on*', and with hundreds of National Guardsmen surrounding the square for security, a crowd numbering fifteen thousand – the largest gathering of blacks in the history of Mississippi – welcomed the marchers. James Meredith, who had sufficiently recovered by now, resumed his place at the head of the march outside Jackson, the state capital. Actors Burt Lancaster, Marlon Brando, and Dick Gregory were some of the luminaries who were also present. Coretta King and King's two older children, Yoke and Marty, also joined King for the final leg of the march from Tougaloo College to the State House.

Amidst a loud applause, McKissick declared, '*(The year) 1966 shall be remembered as the year we left our imposed status as Negroes and became Black men … 1966 is the year of the concept of Black Power.*' Stokley Carmichael exhorted the blacks to '*build a power base … so strong that we will bring (whites) to their knees every time they mess with us.*'

Although there was a massive gathering of blacks, King was far from jubilant. On the contrary, he felt the onset of a weary disillusionment. The rift in the movement was tearing at his heart. This ideological divide was indeed pernicious for the movement. The SCLC, the NAACP and the National Urban League supported integration and non-violence, while the black radicals in the CORE and the SNCC vehemently justified violence and separatism. The alienation of the liberal whites from the movement was also something which he disapproved of. However, he endeavored to end the march on an optimistic note by saying, '*One day, right here in this state of Mississippi, justice will become a reality for all.'* Winding their way through the Mississippi countryside, the marchers sang freedom songs, unlike the earlier marchers. There was palpable defiance in the air, as the songs '*Freedom got a shotgun, freedom got a shotgun, you know freedom gonna shoot it, at these segregated bigots*'.

For some, like James Wechsler, the columnist of the *New York Post*, the growth of *Black Power* was a national tragedy. In the December issue of *The Progressive*, he mourned the fact that the '*killers of the dream are on the offensive ... the evidence is inescapable that the cause of Civil Rights is floundering, all the visions of the Freedom Movement are imperiled, and some deeply dedicated men are helping to set the stage for the destruction of the noblest cause of our time*'.

Although a success in a way, the two-day march dealt a painful blow to King's philosophy of non-violence. '*The old partnership of middle-class Blacks, liberal Whites, and poor Whites was being replaced with the steely vision that Carmichael dubbed Black Power.*'

By now, King was utterly demoralised and disheartened by the rise of the violent ideology of *Black Power.* So he returned to Chicago only to find that hardly any progress had been made, and the city's ghettos were simmering with latent discontent. It was time for more militant non-violent action.

THE CHICAGO FREEDOM MOVEMENT

ON A chokingly hot Sunday, 10 July 1966, with the temperature soaring at 98 degrees Fahrenheit, King initiated a drive to make Chicago an open city, demanding an end to discrimination in schools, housing and employment. Speaking to about 45,000 people on this day, designated as Freedom Sunday, at Soldier's Field, he implored blacks to go to the jails and end slums. He later led thousands of marchers, winding their way through downtown Chicago. Stopping at City Hall, and in a gesture reminiscent of Martin Luther, his 16th Century namesake, they tacked the groups' demands to the door at City Hall, demanding a redress of legitimate grievances.

When black concerns were ignored by Mayor Daley, King followed this up with another march. Soon after this kick-off rally, Chicago's west side erupted in racially-fuelled violence on Tuesday, 12 July 1966, which lasted for two days, finally ending on the third day, when order was restored by about four thousand National Guardsmen.

On Friday, 5 August 1966, he led a large peaceful group of about six hundred marchers out of the ghetto to the Gage

Park district on Chicago's south-western side, while 1,200 policemen stood by. All of a sudden, an irate mob of whites, holding signs, painted with swastikas, symbolic of Hitler's anti-Jewish Germany, started flinging rocks, fire-crackers and racial abuses at them, screaming '*We want Martin Luther Coon*' and '*Kill the Niggers*'.

Hit on the head by a rock, King remarked, '*Oh, I've been hit so many times I'm immune to it.*' Then, in a more serious tone, he said, '*I've been in many demonstrations all across the South, but I can say that I have never seen, even in Mississippi or Alabama, mobs as hostile and hate-filled as I've seen in Chicago.*'

Another march to the Belmont Cragin district, located on the north-western side of Chicago, followed on 7 August 1966, wherein the marchers were stoned by people shouting '*White Power*'.

In Chicago, it was economic dignity that King was trying to tackle and that implied a redistribution of political and economic power, requiring great adjustments in the way of life of the white majority. This demand of the blacks was pitted against the self-interest of white Americans, who were apprehensive that a strong open-housing law would result in a migration of blacks to the suburbs leading to a deterioration of living conditions. Meanwhile, the open-housing demonstrations continued in Chicago, ringing alarm bells for the Daley Machine. The campaign had to be crushed somehow. Mayor Daley's astute mind started whirring.

A ten-hour meeting at the St James Episcopal Church – between the representatives of the City, real estate officials and the Chicago Movement – followed on 17 August 1966, but failed to reach any accord.

Now Daley sought a temporary injunction against these marches, which the City lawyers argued were a '*clear and present danger*'. The Cook County Circuit Court and Judge Cornelius J Harrington ruled against the Chicago Movement, drastically limiting the marches. Not more than five hundred protestors could comprise a march, and there could be only one march per day. Marches were not permitted at night, and between 7.30 am and 9 am in the morning, and between 4.40 pm and 6 pm in the evening. King called this injunction '*unjust, illegal and unconstitutional*'.

Unfazed, he made an announcement that sent shockwaves through the officials. On 28 August 1966, he would lead an inter-racial march into all-white Cicero, a suburb of about 70,000 people outside Cook County, which was beyond the jurisdiction of the injunction.

'Suicidal,' pronounced the Sheriff of Cook County.

'Call the march off,' pleaded the progressive whites, City Hall and Archbishop Cody.

But King was determined that the demonstration would be '*the biggest ever*'. To a crowd at New Liberty Baptist Church, he vowed, '*No one is going to turn me around at this point … Not only are we going to walk to Cicero, we're going to work in Cicero, we're going to live in Cicero.*'

Cicero was the most racist community in the Chicago area. The former residence of gangster Al Capone, it had erupted in racial violence in 1951 when a Negro couple had tried to move there. Order had been restored only when Governor Adlai Stevenson had sent about 4,000 National Guardsmen to control it.

Jerome Huey, a black teenager, had been beaten to death in May 1966 by white youths because he had shown the audacity to seek employment in an area which was supposedly a white bastion.

The federal government and Mayor Daley were afraid that a march to Cicero would unleash a wave of white violence that would be difficult to control, so Mayor Daley frantically started hunting for a way out.

Daley, the shrewd strategist, who had so far succeeded in outflanking King at every step, stoutly denying that anything was wrong with the government's slum policies, was now totally flummoxed. He was forced to arrange a meeting with King, thereby, almost conceding the flawed housing policies. For King and his movement, the sun appeared to be finally peeping through sinister-looking clouds. A major breakthrough had been gained! Negotiations followed between Mayor Daley and King.

On 26 August 1966, Daley announced a '*Summit Agreement*' in which the Chicago Housing Authority promised to build '*non-ghetto, low-rise*' public housing. Regardless of race, the Mortgage Bankers Association agreed to make mortgage available. Moreover, to provide education and direction for the agreement, a permanent body '*The Leadership Council for Metropolitan Open Housing*' would be set up. However, this so-called agreement failed to satisfy many activists, some of whom marched in Cicero on 4 September 1966. To them, it was only a partial compromise, a sell-out, only a series of verbal promises. For King, this agreement was one of the most important programmes ever conceived to make open housing a reality. He agreed that it was '*the first step in a thousand mile journey*'. Non-violence appeared to have won a bottle.

King remarked, '*Never before have such far-reaching and creative commitments been made and programmes adopted and pledged to achieve open housing in a community*'.

Even the media was full of praise for the agreement. In an article titled, '*Still King*', the *Christian Century* eulogised the achievement; the *Chicago Tribune* maintained that the total eradication of housing discrimination has been made possible. For the *Newsweek*, it was a '*solid vindication of Southern style non-violent protest in a Northern city*'. Even Mayor Daley, the consummate politician, who had tried to sabotage the movement at every step, hailed it as a '*great day for the City*'.

However, to many detractors, it was merely '*sound and fury signifying nothing*'. Chester Robinson, the Executive Director of the west-side organisation, condemned it as: '*A lot of words give us nothing specific we can undertake … The situation is just pathetic, we're sick and tired of middle class people telling us what we want. And we're gonna march in Cicero on Sunday.*' Although Robinson cancelled his plans of marching to Cicero, the CORE and SNCC did not. The SNCC and CORE march to Cicero comprised two hundred blacks, protected by ten times as many National Guardsmen, who were assaulted so brutally by racks and bottles that they were forced to flee to Lawndale.

Later, in a victory rally, King gave a frank appraisal of the Chicago movement; '*Let's face the fact. Most of us are going to be living in the ghetto fire ten years from now … Morally, we ought to have what we say in the slogan, "Freedom Now", but it all doesn't come now. That's a sad fact of life you have to live with.*'

There could be no substantial change in the lives of the ghetto residents unless their need for jobs was fulfilled, so now they forged ahead trying to tackle this problem.

OPERATION BREADBASKET

1966-1971

MODELLED AFTER a programme developed by Rev Leon Sullivan in Philadelphia in early 1960s, according to King, '*The fundamental premise of Breadbasket is a simple one. Negroes need not patronise a business which denies them jobs, or advancement, or plain courtesy.*'

More than two hundred ministers attended the kick-off meeting of Chicago's Operation Breadbasket on 11 February 1966. Under Jesse Jackson's leadership, they decided to target milk distribution bakeries, soft drink bottlers and soup companies, forming committees to investigate employment statistics in these industries.

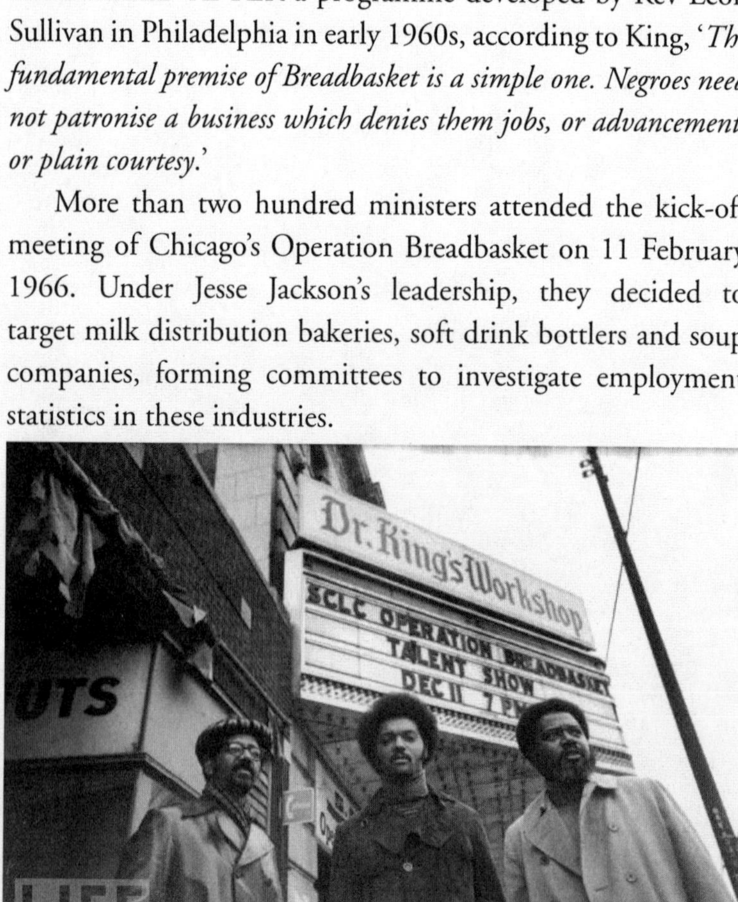

The company *Delight Dairy Product* was the first company to be targeted on the basis of selective patronage. It had to finally comply to their demands, when blacks refused to buy their products and boycotted and picketed the stores that sold them.

In 1967, with the intention of converting Operation Breadbasket into a national organisation, King appointed Jackson as its national director. By 1968, it had successfully conducted more than forty boycotts, which resulted in employment for more than 8,000 African American workers.

Many new projects were undertaken by Operation Breadbasket by the end of the decade. Apart from sponsoring many trade expositions in Chicago, they helped plan the *Poor Peoples' Campaign*, lobbied against welfare cuts, and launched a *free breakfast* programme, also engaged in political campaigns.

The Chicago Freedom Movement sparked off a national debate, leading to the federal Fair Housing Act of 1968. Myriad organisations – Kenwood-Oakland Community Organisation and Leadership Council for Metropolitan Open Communities – tried to address this problem of racial injustice.

Jesse Jackson maintained that King believed that a sustained non-violent movement would take at least three to five years to bring about changes in Chicago. But the newspapers, in their impatience, wanted to make it a three to five-month movement.

The Northern movement, despite its scatter-shot approach,

was able to jerk the comatose Northern black America out of its coma and make it aware of its problems and, as Jackson further emphasised that, as a result of raising certain basic truths in the Chicago movement, Gary Indiana, Newark, New Jersey, Cleveland, Ohio too began to reassess political power and political consciousness.

The *Chicago Freedom Movement* was indeed a milestone in King's life, a crucial transition. 'The rock hit the water in Chicago, but the concentric circles shot right across Northern America, so I think the movement was successful,' was Jesse Jackson's viewpoint.

In a significant new departure, King had shifted from the south to the north in a bid to improve the pathetic condition of the millions of Negroes languishing in ghettos. He had come across certain hurdles that he had not earlier thought of. The racial terrain was different here. Moreover, the local leaders did not approve of King's intrusion into their territory. Black Congressman, William Dawson fumed, 'What does he mean coming in here trying to tell our citizens that we are segregated? Chicagoans know what is best for Chicagoans.' Head of the City Council, Alderman Thomas Keene, said in exasperation, 'King is a disrupter of society. He is trying to disrupt what we built.'

Although they won modest victories here, they had to face obstacles more formidable than those they had encountered in the south. This most ambitious Civil Rights campaign in the north, lasting from mid-1965 to early 1967 in the windy city of Chicago, was not as dazzling as King would have wanted. Some thinkers are of the opinion that the Chicago crusade actually undermined popular support for the movement and that it was a defeat for King and Civil Rights forces.

But the Chicago campaign did produce some positive results. As David Lewis pointed out, 'It was considerably more comprehensive than any of Martin's previous accords. If Birmingham was a triumph, then Chicago certainly ought not to have been assessed as a virtual rout.'

The greatest achievement was that King was finally able to coerce Mayor Daley to the bargaining table. As King put it, '*The whole power structure was forced by the power of the non-violent movement to sit down and negotiate and capitulate and make concessions that have never been made before.*'

The Housing Act of 1968 was passed on 10 April 1968, six days after the assassination of King. But during his lifetime, in-fact during the final year-and-a-half of his life, King was a distraught man, worried that darker days lay ahead. It was indeed a saddened King who realised that most whites did not want the Negro as a brother, and only a miniscule minority of whites believed in racial equality. He sadly wondered whether the racist whites would ever shrug off their racist mindset.

As he had travelled onwards on the trajectory of life from his love-filled home to the hate-filled streets of Chicago, appalled by the viciously distorted maniacal faces jeering at him, calling

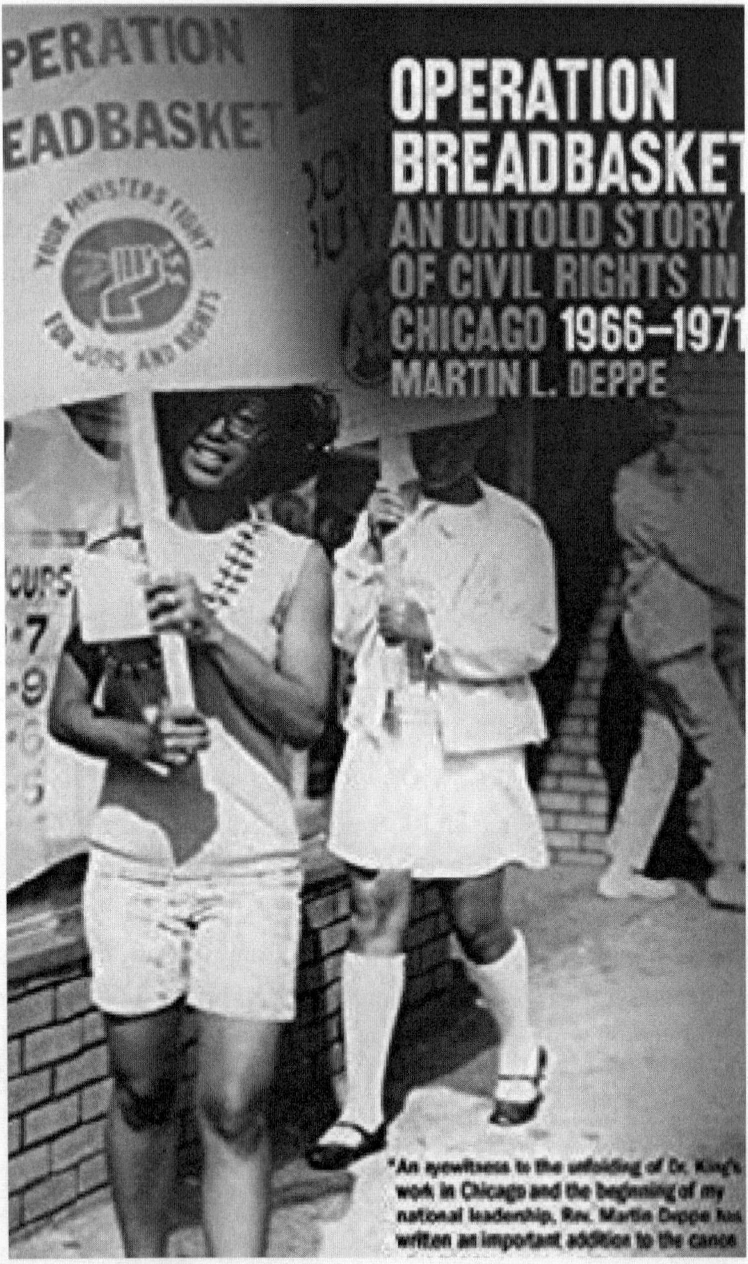
PERATION
EADBASKET
YOUR MINISTERS FIGHT
FOR JOBS AND RIGHTS
OPERATION
BREADBASKE
AN UNTOLD STORY
OF CIVIL RIGHTS IN
CHICAGO 1966–197
MARTIN L. DEPPE
"An eyewitness to the unfolding of Dr. King's
work in Chicago and the beginning of my
national leadership, Rev. Martin Deppe has
written an important addition to the cano

him a nigger and goon, the rock-flinging racists, the bomb-throwing and venom spewing Klansmen, he still could not bring himself to believe that all whites were evil. The lessons in love and non-violence that he had learnt from his parents were etched in his mind. No amount of rock-throwing or epithet-hurling could erase those strongly etched letters of love, non-violence and compassion.

To those of his young friends, who were advocating violence, and quoting their hero Frantz Fanon, a black psychiatrist from Martinique, and author of *The Wretched of The Earth*, who believed that violence for oppressed people was psychologically healthy and tactically sound, King argued, '*Darkness cannot drive out darkness, only light can do that. Hate cannot drive out hate, only love can do that.*'

The Negro community was drifting towards violence, the cry of *Black Power* was resounding in the Negro community, and King was very sad. He said the weakness of *Black Power* is its failure to see that the black man needs the white man and the white man needs the black man.

KING AND THE VIETNAM WAR

THE CAUSE of Civil Rights appeared to be losing momentum and King needed to inject some vigour in his depleting energy. So on 14 January 1967, he flew to Jamaica for a month's holiday hoping to be rejuvenated and to complete the work on his book.

In *Ramparts* magazine, which he had bought at the airport and sat reading on the porch of his Jamaica villa, he read a story about the Vietnam War, with pictures of children who had been maimed or killed by the chemical agent, *napalm*, dropped by the US planes in Vietnam.

Appalled at the sight of rice fields and villages in flames, mothers fleeing blazing huts, kids clutched to their chests, American and Vietnamese soldiers with their limbs and faces blown away, and burned and disfigured bodies of Vietnamese children, he felt that '*a war that incinerated children was a war that mutilated his conscience*'.

His passionate and brilliant lieutenant, James Bevel, the SCLC Project Director, left his post to take over as the Executive Director of the Spring Mobilisation Committee, which aimed to end the war in Vietnam. He also exhorted King to join forces with him, trying to convince him about the monstrosity of war.

In his cliffside phoneless villa, King slogged for twelve to fourteen hours a day trying to meet the Harper and Row deadline of 15 February 1967. During breaks in his writing, he mulled over the war, strongly convinced that if America ceased the killing, it could utilise the money thus saved in transforming many a life.

On returning from Jamaica, as he sat before his television set, horrifying images from the Vietnam War flashed before his eyes, jerking him out of his complacence. He told Andrew Young and Stanley Levison that he had decided to oppose the war. The Vietnam War was a colossal drain on the money, manpower and energy that could be successfully utilised in their crusade against poverty. Talking to his friends he said, '*I can't be silent. Never again will I be silent.*'

And he was not silent.

On 25 February 1967, in a conference sponsored by *The Nation* in Los Angeles, he launched an assault on American foreign policy, arguing that American policy could only lead to '*national disaster*'. Passion pouring forth from every word, he said:

'*The bombs in Vietnam explode at home; they destroy the hopes and possibilities for a decent America. I speak out against it, not in anger, but with anxiety and sorrow in my heart and, above all, with a passionate desire to see our beloved country stand as the moral example of the world… we must combine the fervour of the Civil Rights movement with the peace movement… we must demonstrate, teach and preach until the very foundations of our nation are shaken.*'

Now, King was full throttle on the anti-war trail, while the FBI was in hot pursuit, and his detractors, even amongst the Negroes accused him of betraying the cause of Civil Rights, but King had made up his mind, silence at this juncture could be criminal. The Vietnam War, to him, was like '*some demoniacal destructive suction tube*' insanely drawing '*men, skills and money*', devastating the hopes of the poor, and cruelly manipulating them.

On 25 March 1967, at a rally in the Chicago Coliseum, he

reiterated the merging of the Civil Rights and peace movements. Within a week, approving King's radical stand, the SCLC also condemned the war as '*morally and politically unjust*'.

Much to President Johnson's anger and embarrassment, King became an outspoken critic of the Vietnam War. Citing several reasons for '*bringing Vietnam into the field of my moral vision*', he staunchly maintained that he could no longer maintain his neutrality. Dante's words preyed on his turbulent head: '*The hottest places in hell are reserved for those who, in a moment of moral crisis, seek to maintain their neutrality*'. He had to shake off his neutrality, ignore the hostility of the supporters of the war and, with his impassioned eloquence, make America listen.

On the evening of 4 April 1967, King delivered a very powerful speech at the Riverside Church in New York, under the auspices of clergy and laymen, which concerned with the Vietnam War.

Some consider this speech greater than his '*I have a dream*' speech.

The moment he rose to speak, he received a thunderous applause. His baritone swept across the Church:

'Over the past two years, as I have moved to break the betrayal of my own silences and to speak from the burnings of my own heart ... many persons have questioned me about the wisdom of my path ... Why are (you) speaking about the war? Dr King why are you joining the voices of dissent; Peace and Civil Rights don't mix, they say, "Aren't you hurting the cause of your people?", they ask.'

He reiterated: '*The highly promising Poverty Programme had been broken and eviscerated, as if it were some idle political plaything of a society gone mad on war, and I knew that America would never invest the necessary funds or energies in rehabilitation of its poor so long as adventures, like Vietnam, continued ...*'

His mesmerising oration dominated the meeting that clear and crisp night, as he poured passion in his words:

'*We must move past indecision to action. We must find new ways to speak for peace in Vietnam and justice throughout the developing world – a world that borders on our doors. If we do not act, we shall surely be dragged down the long dark and shameful corridors of time reserved for those who possess power without compassion, might without morality and strength without sight.'*

Through his passionate eloquence, he had really succeeded in making the three thousand people, who had filled the Riverside Church that night, listen to the '*broken cries of the people who have been living under the curse of war for almost three continuous decades now.*'

With this speech, King ceased to be only a Negro leader. He stood on the international stage, convincingly stating his case for a new world based on non-violence, peace, compassion and redemptive love.

Racial Riots

King continued to denounce the war with a passionate intensity, as President Johnson continued to grow more belligerent, and the war continued to escalate. A war-obsessed

President Johnson spoke against King, wrathful at the '*Dump Johnson*' campaign within the Democratic Party, and absolutely convinced that the peace movements spearheaded by King were being financed by Red China.

In the meantime, racial tension escalated, as the ghetto blacks revolted against an unjust system, where they had been denied the basic rights.

The long, hot summer became hotter, as violence flared up in Boston's Roxbury district and for five horrifying days and nights Cincinnati was engulfed in flames.

Roxbury (Boston), June 1967

Roxbury, Boston's predominantly Negro section, was comparatively peaceful, working its way through myriad programmes in the spheres of job training, education, recreation, welfare, and sanitation with a placid steadiness. But then things changed suddenly on 2 June 1967, unleashing a wave of violence, which took everyone by surprise.

On this day, a Friday, *Mothers For Adequate Welfare* (MAW) were demonstrating at the Grove Hall office, in Roxbury, but since their grievances had not yet been considered and the office had to be closed for the weekend, they decided to shut the double set of exit doors to the building, inviting the wrath of five policemen. Welfare workers were trapped inside the building, and outside the police officers tried to tackle the demonstrators with guns, billy clubs and baseball bats. They were beaten and thrown into paddy wagons. On the very first day, there was damage to the tune of $500,000.

Women and children who were trapped inside the hall were viciously bludgeoned and those outside could not bear to remain quiet. The nocturnal heat, the brutality of the police and a furious crowd were elements that further sparked the riot. Moreover, the Boston Negroes were gradually becoming aware of the Civil Rights activities and the antipoverty programme in other parts of the country. In the changed circumstances, they could ill-afford to be mute spectators, apathetic to the injustice around them.

Despite appeals for calm by various groups, the violence raged on, there were scattered outbursts throughout the evening which petered out, as dawn approached. By 5 June 1967, the violence had subsided to a great extent, although sporadic outbursts still continued.

Although the police and the mayor held the criminal elements responsible for this violence, the youth felt that this was an opportunity that they had been hoping for and praying for all along. United against a common cause, the youngsters resolved to throw bricks until winter arrived, and then snowballs in winter. The Roxbury riots stopped momentarily, only to erupt with a greater vengeance.

Newark (New Jersey), July 1967

Housing segregation had begun in Newark in 1870, when the blacks had started moving to Newark, concentrating the community into one of the nation's poorest ghettoes. Factors like substandard housing, the second highest rate of crime and infant mortality, high unemployment, inferior schools, a lack of political power, a corrupt municipal government combined to escalate the racial tension in Newark.

The worst rioting since the Watts rebellion (1965) occurred in Brick City, Newark, the largest city in New Jersey. It began with the arrest of John Smith, an African cab driver who reportedly drove around a double-parked police car at the corner of 7th Street and 15th Avenue. He was brutalised by the police officers after his arrest and incarcerated at the 4th precinct police headquarters. This unleashed a surge of violence, exacerbated by a rumour that he had fallen a victim to police brutality when actually he had been taken to a local hospital from the backdoor.

Many residents migrated to the neighbouring suburbs, as a result of these riots, permanently changing the face of Newark. These riots lasted for 5 days – 12 to 17 July 1967 – leaving 26 dead, including the 10-year-old Edward Moses. It caused a damage of about $10 million to property. Many kids were hidden in bath tubs by their mothers to protect them from stray bullets.

Detroit Riots, July 1967

Detroit was converted into a gruesome inferno. In fact, police brutality was the one major problem that led to the riot followed by 'poor housing.'

By the end of the 1950s, the youth of Detroit were filled with a hopeless despair, as de-industrialisation was playing havoc with them. This internationally-recognised centre of automobile production was economically better off than other American industrial cities in the post-war era. But at the beginning of the 1950s, Chrysler, GM and Ford took to outsourcing the production of parts to foreign countries and subcontractors of other municipalities. This was a great blow to the young blacks with pent-up frustration and indignation, and finally found an outlet on the streets of Detroit in the early morning hours of Sunday, 23 July 1967. The immediate cause was the raid by the police on an unlicensed bar on 12th Street and Clairmount on the city's west side. What followed was a most deadly, destructive and devastating race riot in the US history. Theft, vandalism and looting reigned supreme for five days – 23 to 27 July 1967.

After some initial dilly-dallying, the Johnson administration authorised the use of federal troops, shortly before midnight on 24 July 1967, giving Detroit the dubious distinction of being the first and only city ever to be occupied by federal troops three times.

On 25 July 1967, a disillusioned King shot a telegram to President Johnson:

'*The chaos and destruction which now spreads through our cities is a blind revolt against the revolting conditions which you so courageously set out to remedy as you entered office in 1964. The conditions have not changed.*'

The four-day holocaust in Detroit, which killed 43 people, including 33 black people, and destroyed property worth $50 million was '*the externalisation of the Negro's inner torrent and rage*'.

Accusing the administration of 'moral degradation', King warned that the '*hypocrisy and confusion seeping through the fabric of society can ultimately destroy from within the very positive values of our nation which no enemy could destroy from without*'.

His passionate plea to President Johnson to 'establish justice' immediately fell on deaf ears and Johnson admonished the Negroes, asking them to follow the law. Indignantly, King asked, *'How can the administration, with quivering anger, denounce the violence of ghetto Negroes when it has given an example of violence in Asia that shocks the world... only those who are fighting for peace have the moral authority to lecture on non-violence.'*

Finally, order was restored to the city by Thursday, 27 July 1967, and troops started withdrawing on Friday, 28 July 1967. By 29 July 1967, the federal troops were completely withdrawn.

Black and white people – ranging in age between 68-year-old George Messerlian, a white man, who was killed while defending his shoe repair shop, and 4-year-old Tanya Blanding, a black kid, who died as a result of gunfire from a National Guard Tank stationed in front of her house – were all victims to gory mindlessness!

These riots opened up wide cleavages between the blacks and the whites, putting Detroit on the path to economic desolation.

In 1968, the London Free Press reported that Detroit was '*a sick city, where fear, rumour, race, prejudice and gun-buying have stretched the Black and White nerves to the verge of snapping*'.

The Kerner Commission

A National Advisory Commission on Civil Disorders, chaired by Illinois Governor, Otto Kerner Jr was appointed by President Johnson on 28 July 1967 to look into the reasons for the riots, and to suggest remedial measures. This 11-member Commission, after seven months of investigation, issued its report on 29 February 1968, stating:

'Our nation was moving towards two societies, one Black and one White – separate and unequal.'

Without mincing any words, it frankly admitted that it was white racism that was responsible for the deplorable condition of the ghettoes; it were the white institutions that had created and maintained it; and it was the white society that condoned it. It categorically maintained that the democratic values of America would start eroding if drastic remedies were not taken immediately to correct the imbalance.

'The press has too long basked in a White world, looking out of it, if at all, with White men's eyes and White perspectives.'

This 426-page document was hailed by King as a '*physician's warning of approaching death, with a prescription of life*'.

POOR PEOPLE'S CAMPAIGN

THE CACOPHONY of hate and violence that was spreading in the ghettoes, was callousing King's eardrums. All along he had been pleading for non-violence and sanity, but now America appeared to be teetering on the brink of disaster. The whites and the blacks were hopelessly polarised, the whites arguing that the violence in the ghettos had 'cremated' non-violence.

H Rap Brown, successor to Stokley Carmichael as SNCC chairman in 1967, said that violence is as American as cherry pie. He later threatened: 'If America doesn't come around, we're going to burn America down.'

Time was now ripe for mobilising a nation.

Earlier, they had mobilised one city at a time, but now, exigencies of the circumstances were crying out for action on a larger scale, the pathetic condition of the poor of America, both black and white, were screaming for attention. King was yearning for another march to Washington, this time to compel the unwilling authorities to yield to the mandates of justice.

The non-violent method had borne rich dividends in the south, now he was moving from Civil Rights to Human

Rights, acutely aware of the need for a better distribution of wealth, which he believed could also be tackled by the method of non-violence.

At Crozer Theological Seminary, he had been impressed by the ideas of the social Gospel movement. Walter Rauschenbusch's *Christianity and the Social Crisis* (1907) had made him realise that any religion which professes to be concerned about the souls of men but is not concerned about the social and economic conditions that scar the soul is a spiritually moribund religion.

Until the end of his life, King was fully convinced that poverty, racial justice and the war were all inextricably bound together. Poverty was now his focal issue.

On 16 August 1967, in his address to the tenth anniversary convention of the SCLC, King maintained '*one day we must come to see that an edifice which produces beggars needs restructuring*'. He remarked: '*America, you must be born again!*'

Denouncing both capitalism and communism, he advocated Christian democratic socialism, which can establish economic programmes to fulfill the needs of all people, irrespective of race. Motivated by Christian values, King maintained it can even foster the *Kingdom of Brotherhood.*

Issues of poverty had been tackled by many academicians and writers prior to King's campaign against poverty; they had all maintained that poverty was an all-pervasive phenomenon in America, which was detrimental for the nation.

Gunnar Myrdal, in *An American Dilemma* (1944), reiterated that many Americans continued to be trapped in a vicious cycle of poverty, pathetically lagging behind others. Kenneth

Galbraith, in *The Affluent Society* (1958), declared that massive inequality was dangerous for democracy. Michael Harrington, in his bestselling book *The Other America* (1962), depicted the plight of those 40 to 50 million people living in poverty.

Issues of poverty had only mildly interested President Kennedy, his priorities being the cold war and foreign policy. No urgency was felt to implement poverty alleviation programmes. It was only after his assassination that his aides felt this urgency. His successor, President Johnson, inspired by the *New Deal* programme of President Roosevelt, launched the *War on Poverty* programme in January 1964, to be followed by the passage of the *Economic Opportunity Act* in August 1964.

At the Democratic National Convention on 27 August 1964, President Johnson declared loftily: 'For More than 30 years, from social security to war against poverty, we have diligently worked to enlarge the freedom of man.' But alas, these words had a hollow ring. Soon, the programmes of poverty alleviation became controversial. Johnson's paternalistic mindset came to the fore.

America's involvement in the Vietnam War was the proverbial last nail in the coffin of the war on poverty initiative. Added to it was FBI Director J Edgar Hoover's campaign to condemn King's attempts – at securing economic justice for the Negroes – as communist influence.

In June 1964, King's book *Why We Can't Wait* was published and one analyst called it a 'searing indictment of economic racism'.

Now, the issue of economic justice was uppermost in King's mind and in his acceptance speech for the 1964 Nobel

Peace prize, King spoke about the problem of poverty: '*I am mindful that debilitating and grinding poverty afflicts my people and chains them to the lowest rung of the economic ladder.*'

King was bent on unshackling the poor from the bondage of poverty and pushing them up the economic ladder. He said:

'*What we are seeing now is a freedom explosion, the realisation of "an idea whose time has come" to use Victor Hugo's phrase. The deep rumbling of discontent that we hear today is the thunder of disinherited masses, rising from dungeons of oppression to the bright hills of freedom, in one majestic chorus, the rising masses singing, in the words of our freedom song, "Ain't gonna let nobody turn us around."*'

Malcolm X also prodded the administration for 'better food, clothing, housing, education and jobs right now', though his methods of reaching that goal differed from King's. Moreover, the media was also expressing its deep concern over the problem of poverty.

It was against this backdrop that King launched the *Poor People's Campaign*, with the promise that the poor would be acknowledged in the richest nation of the world. Through this ambitious project, he hoped to reach across apparently, impenetrable racial, cultural, ethnic lines that divided the nation's poor. Undaunted by the Herculean task of forging this multi-ethnic alliance and, at the same time, striking a balance between myriad objectives, King was on the verge of breaking new ground.

Despite a clamour of demands for far-reaching reforms in the socio-economic field, the federal government had failed to respond. So, it was time to confront this indifferent and callous government that was brutalising the poor people in America, and turning a blind eye to the pathetic condition of the poor in the ghettos torn asunder by riots. Now, a determined King was out '*to cripple the operations of an oppressive society*'.

A monumental campaign was in the offing, and the staffers of SCLC were apprehensive. Where was the wherewithal? Where were the funds? Wouldn't the government try to sabotage their plans?

But King's mind had been made up. He said:

'We are going to reach out to the poor people in all directions in this country. We're going into the South West after the Indians, into the West after the Chicanos, into Appalachia after the poor whites, and into the ghettos after Negroes and Puerto Ricans. And we're going to bring them together and enlarge this campaign into something bigger than just a Civil Rights movement for Negroes.'

James Bevel, one of his own lieutenants, had vociferously opposed such a campaign, arguing that SCLC's major thrust must be against the war; peace was far more important than a movement aimed at domestic economic issues. Much to King's chagrin, Bevel had denounced the whites as the most 'savage, bestial, corrupt, murderous people on earth, and they engage in war games, killing, tricking all the time. They can't help that. It's not because they are mean. It's because they are mentally ill'. He wanted an all-out peace offensive that would tell the truth about the white people of America.

Although personally supporting an all-out peace offensive, King was emphatic that it was high time something was done about the serious problem of economic oppression and war was also a part of the *whole problem of economic exploration.* He said he would *'stay in jail six months, if necessary'*, and vowed: '*Federal authorities* aren't *going to run me out of Washington. America is at a crossroads of history.'*

King warned a crowded press conference at Ebenezer Baptist Church in Atlanta on 4 December 1967: '*It is critically important for us, as a nation and a society, to choose a new path and move upon it with resolution and courage. It is impossible to underestimate the crisis we face in America*.'

The new path that King had chosen was a 'strong, dramatic, and attention-getting campaign' of mass civil disobedience in Washington DC, which would aim at forcing the federal government to guarantee jobs for all Americans, and eradicating the deplorable slums once and for all.

This campaign would begin in April 1968, for after all, '*the stability of a civilisation, the potential of free government and the simple honour of men, are at stake*'.

For King, this was his last greatest dream, a desperate attempt to prove the detractors wrong, and a moral responsibility to a nation to prove that non-violence was not dead, and writing elegies for its death was a little too premature. Firmly convinced that government inaction would spell doom for America, and that the stability of a civilisation, the potential of free government, and the simple honour of men are at stake, he outlined his plan.

SCLC would recruit three thousand poor people from five rural areas and ten major cities, train them in the techniques of non-violence for three months and then bring them to Washington to disrupt transportation and government operations.

In a SCLC meeting in January 1968, in Miami, Florida, King secured the official SCLC approval for his Washington spring project. Bayard Rustin, his personal adviser, stoutly opposed him:

'Given the mood in Congress, given the increasing backlash across the nation, given the fact that this is an election year, and given the high visibility of a protest movement in the national capital, I feel that in this atmosphere, any effort to disrupt transportation, government building etc, can only lead to further backlash and repression.'

Rustin further warned: 'You are attempting the impossible. There is no way for Martin Luther King to bring white poor, Puerto Rican poor, black poor, Irish poor together in any meaningful way.'

Although wary about his forthcoming project, King was stubbornly optimistic about pulling it off, although the odds were stacked heavily against him. He launched a recruitment drive in mid-January 1968, dispatching forty SCLC field workers to rural areas in the South and to Baltimore, New York, Boston, Cleveland, Detroit, Philadelphia, and Newark. Bernard Lafayette J, a former SNCC field secretary and a new SCLC officer, was entrusted with the responsibility of directing the campaign. He followed this with a promotional tour on the west coast, spreading his message along the way.

The poor response to the *Poor People's Campaign* was creating havoc with King's psyche, making him distraught, *what-if* questions plagued his mind, giving him sleepless nights.

It was in such a frame of mind that he delivered the touching message to the Negro People of Ebenezer on 4 February 1968, the poignant message, the tape of which would be played two months later on 9 April 1968, at his memorial service at Ebenezer Baptist Church.

'If any of you are around when I have to meet my day, I don't want a long funeral ... I'd like somebody to mention that day, that Martin Luther King Jr tried to give his life serving others. I'd like for somebody to say that day that Martin Luther King Jr tried to love somebody. I want you to say that day that I tried to be right on the war question. I want you to be able to say that day that I did try to feed the hungry ... to clothe those who were naked ... to love and serve humanity ...'

Although utterly distraught, he had the resilience and the faith to go on. Bent on unifying Washington Negroes behind his project, he was keen that the militant Negroes should also give non-violence a chance, and with this aim King flew to Washington two days after this historic sermon and met the SNCC chairman, H Rap Brown, and Stokley Carmichael in a secret meeting in a Washington motel.

Although he did not want any rabid elements involved in the campaign, he was hopeful that the SNCC, which had been racked by internal dissension, and which had an anti-white stance could be persuaded to come round to his way of thinking, for, as King stated, *'We still believe in black and white together and, therefore, we need this movement. We need to bring about a new kind of togetherness between blacks and whites. We need it to bring allies together and to bring the coalition of conscience together.'*

A fiercely determined King started a people-to-people tour, travelling thousands of miles and meeting leaders of various ethnic groups, his aim being to recruit volunteers, ensure financial wherewithal and to reassure the poor – both black and white – that power for poor people meant developing '*the ability, togetherness, the assertiveness, and the aggressiveness to make the power structure respond*'.

Hoping that the poor of all hues and shades would march to Washington with him, he interacted with Negroes and Puerto Ricans Indians and Chicanos in the South, the South-west and the far East.

In his Nobel Peace Prize lecture, on 11 December 1964, King had reiterated the need for a life of dignity and worth, and for launching an all-out world war against poverty. There was a crying need to '*develop the underdeveloped, school the unschooled, and feed the unfed*'.

He had pointed out that it was the responsibility of the wealthy nations to '*bridge the gulf between the rich minority and the poor majority*'.

Poverty, he maintained, was a *monstrous octopus*, which was projecting '*its nagging, prehensile tentacles in lands and villages all over the world. Almost two-thirds of the peoples of the world go to bed hungry at night. They are undernourished, ill-housed and shabbily clad. Many of them have no houses or beds to sleep in. Their only beds are the side-walks of the cities and the dusty roads of the villages. Most of the poverty-stricken children of God have never seen a physician or a dentist*'.

Quoting John Donne, he had said:

"*Any man's death diminishes me, because I am involved in Mankinde: and therefore never send to know for whom the bell tolls: it tolls for thee.*" (Final Lines of *Devotions,* 1624)

The *Poor People's Campaign* was a campaign launched by King in response to his personalistic leanings, which told him time and again that an attack on one person is an attack on the entire humanity. The plight of one shirtless and barefooted person was an assault on every other person. Unless the poor folks were *'lifted from the long night of poverty, illiteracy and disease'*, the dignity of entire humanity was at stake.

The idea of such a campaign received adverse criticism from different quarters. It was labelled as unwise and untimely even by the Negro leaders. The liberal whites were afraid that such a march would engulf Washington in flames. The media went all out in condemning the planned movement. *The Atlanta Constitution*, commented that 'paralysing a city's economy and movement hardly sounds like the redemptive suffering Dr King used to speak of'.

'How dare King bring a Negro army to protest against him; hadn't he done a lot for the Negroes?' President Johnson fumed and even tried to force King into calling off the campaign. On his refusal, King was accused of criminal disobedience against the government.

Johnson thundered that he would not permit lawlessness 'in whatever form and in whatever guise'.

The FBI launched a vicious campaign against him, accusing King of embezzlement, of leaning towards communism, and of personal transgressions. He was scorned, cursed and berated, stalked and ridiculed for daring to launch a movement which could only be counter productive.

George Schuyler, a black writing in a column in the *St Louis Globe Democrat,* maintained that King and his peripatetic parsons were plotting a new racial war and the President had no plans to preside over the liquidation of the American nation or sit fiddling in the White House, while Washington burns.

King was at the receiving end of a hate campaign unleashed by the Klan, and was distraught that his relationship with President Johnson had become acrimonious.

Despite his vulnerable state, and the threats to his life, King refused to carry a gun or let anyone of his colleagues do so. Ever since his house had been bombed on 30 January 1956 and his wife and daughter Yoki had narrowly escaped death, and angry Negroes had surrounded his house crying for revenge, he had calmed the vindictive crowd with the words, '*We must love our White brothers, no matter what they do to us... we must meet hate with love.*' That night he had been torn with a corroding hatred for those who had tried to bomb his house.

Though his saner sense tried to counsel him against bitterness, he had later gone to the sheriff's house and applied for a gun permit, only to realise soon, the wrongness of his action.

He emerged from the crisis, a true Gandhian who had no need for any gun, even for self defence. The six-year-old, who '*was determined to hate every White person*' because of the indignities of racial discrimination that he had suffered, had completely deleted the word *hatred* from his lexicon by the time he was twenty seven.

Now, as a thirty-eight-year-old, he was completely purged of hatred for any person or community. Whether it was the hate campaign of the Klan or the vicious campaign of the FBI, or Johnson's salvoes against him or the threats to his life, he strongly believed in the redemptive power of love and non-violence.

He tried to squeeze a lifetime into each day, apprehensive that death lurked in every dark corner, but no, he was not afraid of death. If there was one fear that he had conquered, it was the fear of death.

Although he tried to put up a brave front, the strain was creating havoc in his mind, alarming Coretta and his colleagues, who suggested that he should slacken his pace and consult psychiatrists.

The *Poor People's Campaign* aimed at bringing full democracy to America, changing the nation up to a point that it would be forced to live up to its creed. The immediate purpose of this *mammoth job* was to coerce Congress into enacting King's proposed $12 billion *Bill of Rights* for the disadvantaged, an end to housing discrimination, jobs for those who could work, and a regular income for those who couldn't.

Despite the initial reservations from his inner circle, and his own qualms and doubts, by mid-March 1968, a cautious hope appeared to replace hopelessness. Many religious organisations promised support in many important areas. There was a spurt in volunteers and even the NAACP threw in its lot with the SCLC.

In his people-to-people tours, King heard heart-wrenching stories of poverty and deprivation, which brought him close to tears. He was warmly greeted by admiring crowds wherever he went.

It was with a renewed sense of energy that he tried to balance idealism with reality. The lofty ideal of the American Dream could be realised only when the frustration and desperation entrenched in America's poor could be abolished, only when the '*two societies, one Black, one White – separate and unequal*' could become one and equal.

Was such an idea a wild-goose chase or an exercise in futility? This is what the detractors persistently and relentlessly maintained, saying that it was too ambitious and its demands too amorphous. But as King emphatically maintained on 17 January 1968, in a staff meeting, that it was '*possible, so achievable, so pure, so simple*'.

Although inherently different from the other campaigns that the SCLC had launched earlier, King declared that '*it's as pure as a man needing an income to support his family*'. Surely that wasn't too ambitious?

The master plan for the Washington campaign was completed by 12 February 1968.

The Phase I would commence in late April, whereby an initial force of several thousand poor people would march to Washington, encamp in a visible shanty town and try to highlight – in a dramatic manner – the pathetic condition of the poor of America, irrespective of colour, class and creed. King even mulled over the feasibility of a mule train from Mississippi to Washington, with the aim of dramatising their plight.

[After King's death, those who tried to fulfill his dream of the campaign also tried to experiment with the idea of the mule train and these caravans of the mule train became one of the major highlights of the campaign, which were enthusiastically received in the cities that they passed.]

In Phase II, the poor people's army would launch a two-pronged attack – disruption and dislocation, being its aim. It would disrupt government operations through non-violent sit-ins, a reminiscent of Gandhi's non-cooperation movement against

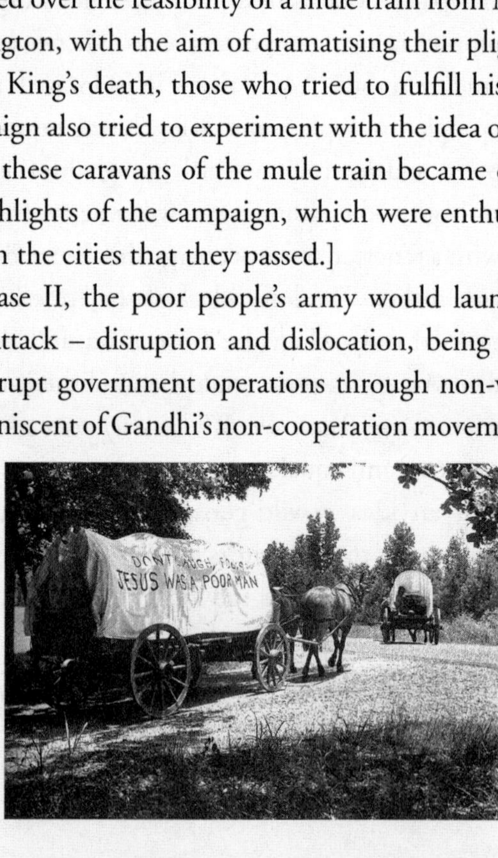

the British government. In typical Gandhian spirit, they would get themselves arrested, to be soon replaced by more demonstrators recruited from colleges and the Washington ghetto.

It was King's earnest dream that these non-violent warriors willingly courting arrest, and making the jails burst, not only with their physical presence, but also their fervour, would succeed in arousing 'a moribund, insensitive Congress to life'.

For a period of three months or more, they would put pressure on the Congress, shaming it into accepting the miserable condition of the poor and grant them 'Economic Bill of Rights'.

It was his aim '*to dramatise the gulf between promise and fulfillment, to call attention to the gap between the dream and the realities, to make the invisible visible. All too often in the rush of everyday life, there is a tendency to forget the poor, to overlook the poor, to allow the poor to become invisible ...*'

In Phase III, it was their intention to take the problems of the poor from the periphery to the very heart of the economic system. Bent on pricking the conscience of America, King was not unaware of the pitfalls involved, but nevertheless, he would forge ahead with his plan if Congress did not listen to their pleas.

Selected industries and shopping centers in big cities would be boycotted, backed up by continued demonstrations and arrests in Washington and other parts of the country. They would also resort to sit-ins at factories, which would coerce businessmen to pressurise Congress into accepting their demands.

The Congress had to make a choice between agreeing to their demands or facing more devastating riots, and King was convinced that they would eventually overcome all hurdles and emerge victorious.

During all these days, King was under a tremendous strain although he tried to appear calm in his public appearances. In the middle of February 1968, he went to Jamaica with Andrew Young and Coretta, and later with his friend and confidante, Ralph Abernathy, to Acapulco, where to Abernathy's intense horror, he behaved in a very strange manner, as though something was troubling him, and even told him what he expected him to do with the SCLC.

But then, like, the *karma yogi* Gandhi, King, managed to marshal his inner resources and moral strength, refusing to cow down under the strain, emphatically maintaining that he would remain an eternal optimist, with his feet firmly planted in reality.

King and Du Bois

On 23 February 1968, he appeared in Carnegie Hall to pay a tribute to WEB Du Bois, on his 100th birth anniversary. Speaking of him, he said, '*He confronted the establishment as a model of militant manhood and integrity. He defied them and though they heaped venom and scorn on him, his powerful voice was never still.*'

William Edward Burghardt Du Bois was popularly known by his initials WEB Du Bois. He was born on 23 Feb 1868 and died on 27 August 1963 at the ripe old age of 95, during which he espoused the cause of universal racial harmony and demanded full Civil Rights for blacks, trying to promote Pan-Africanism.

In 1909, he co-founded the NAACP – *National Association for the Advancement of Colored People* – and for 25 years, this towering black intellectual was the editor-in-chief of *Crisis* magazine, the main artery for distributing the NAACP policy, who flung salvoes at the whites for perpetuating their oppression against the blacks.

About him eminent historian David Levering Lewis wrote:

> In the course of his long turbulent career, W.E.B. Du Bois attempted virtually every possible solution to the problem of twentieth century racism – scholarship, propaganda, integration, national self-determination, human rights, cultural and economic separatism, politics, international communism, expatriation, third world solidarity.

Both King and Du Bois received a magnanimous share of venom and scorn but, like Du Bois, King, the indomitable warrior that he was, never allowed his powerful baritone to be still; to him, silence in the face of injustice, was treachery.

In late February 1968, commenting on the Kerner Commission Report, King declared that the duty of every '*American is to administer the remedy without regard for the cost and without delay*'.

But President Johnson had other priorities; he felt that the United States could ill-afford to implement the Kerner proposals because they involved an expenditure of $30 billion.

An outraged Robert Kennedy fumed: 'This means he's not going to do anything about the war and he's not going to do anything about the cities either.'

Despite tall claims of repeated victories in the Vietnam

War, there was solid proof that President Johnson's claims were vacuous. This intensified the *Dump Johnson* campaign within the Democratic Party and King remarked that Johnson '*seemed amazingly devoid of statesmanship*'.

To the utter surprise of political analysts, Eugene McCarthy – the US Senator from Minnesota – almost defeated Johnson in the New Hampshire primary on 12 March 1968. Robert Kennedy also jumped into the fray four days later.

Organising and planning for the campaign was in full swing when circumstances forced King to make a detour to Memphsis where the striking sanitation workers needed his physical presence and moral support.

SANITATION WORKERS STRIKE – I AM A MAN

ON 1 FEBRUARY 1968, two black sanitation workers – Echol Cole and Robert Walker – were crushed to death in Memphis, Tennessee, when the compactor mechanism of a trash truck was accidentally triggered during a torrential rainstorm.

On the same day, in an incident of unfair discrimination, twenty-two black sewer workers were sent home without pay due to the bad weather, while the white supervisors were retained with pay. This was a great blow to the self-esteem of the blacks, who, as it is, were already labouring under pathetically low wages, humiliating poverty, bad working conditions, disproportionately high mortality rates, and a highly segregated school system. Their plight was further aggravated with the decline of factory employment for blacks. Moreover, the election of Mayor Henry Loeb, a Republican fiscal conservative, in a city of around 540,000 people, forty per cent of whom were blacks, was indicative of the fact that the whites were not serious about establishing racial equality.

Galvanised into immediate action, the black sanitation workers of Memphis established a local chapter of *American Federation of State County and Municipal Employees* (AFSCME) and wanted the city to grant them a contract for improvement of wages, working conditions and recognition of their union. But their demands fell on deaf ears.

Holding aloft placards, which proclaimed *I am a Man*, around 1,300 black sanitation workers went on strike on 12 February 1968. These placards became well known icons of the Civil Rights era. When the police assaulted them, the outraged black community organised a strike-support group, called Community on the Move for Equality (COME), and started daily marches from Mason Temple to City Hall. The city secured a local court injunction against further marches and an intransigent Mayor Henry Loeb threatened them with dire consequences if they did not return to their jobs.

James Lawson, an old friend and pastor of the Centenary Methodist Church in Memphis, pleaded with King to come to Memphsis and address the sanitation workers. He felt King's presence would definitely give a fillip to their movement.

King thought over Lawson's plea and decided to go to Memphis, as their strike appeared similar to the kind of campaign they were planning themselves for Washington. To his staff, he said: *These are poor folks, if we don't stop for them, then we don't need to go to Washington. These are part of the people we're going there for.*

Accordingly, rescheduling his programme, he flew to Memphis on 18 March 1968 along with his staff and checked into Lorraine Hotel where 16 days later, he would fall victim to a sniper's bullet.

Around 17,000 people gave him a warm welcome. Robust cries of '*Yes, Sir*' and '*awright*', and stamping and shouting followed the passionate words that flowed from his mouth, reminiscent of the movement's hey days: *You have assembled for more than thirty days now, to say we are tired. We are tired of being at the bottom … We are tired of having to live in dilapidated, substandard housing. We are tired of working our hands off and laboring every day and not even making a wage adequate with the daily basic necessities of life. We are tired of our men being emasculated, so that our wives and daughters have to go out and work in the white ladies kitchens.*

There was a spontaneous outpouring of love from the audience. Exuberant cries greeted him as he forged ahead with his vibrant persuasive appeal: '… *and so I say, we're not gonna let any dogs or water hoses turn us around. We aren't gonna let any injunction turn us around. We've gotta march again in order to put the issue where it is supposed to be, force everybody to see that thirteen hundred of God's Children are suffering, sometimes going hungry.*'

He told the applauding, singing crowd that there would be a massive downtown non-violent march on Friday, 22 March 1968, and he promised to lead it. He beseeched all black employees to boycott their jobs and all black students to stay away from schools that day. The flagging spirits were revived and the nation's attention was now riveted on Memphis. Their enthusiasm thrilled him. Snug in the knowledge of their love and zeal, he headed back to Mississippi, totally ignorant of a group of *Black Power* youth in Memphis who were bent on launching an assault on the established black leadership and its non-violent approach. They quoted Rap Brown who said that blacks '*must move from resistance to aggression, from revolt to revolution*'.

There was a strong undercurrent of sympathy for their ideology among some of the city youth. As King was unaware of it, he did not make any arrangements for an eventuality where these militant youths would try to sabotage their non-violent plans. Returning to Mississippi, he resumed his people to people tour.

'When the berry season comes, we pick berries; when the rabbit season comes, we hunt and catch a few rabbits; and that's about it.' This was how an impoverished parent answered when, during the *people-to-people* tour, in a town called Mark, King saw naked poverty face to face, and asked one of the parents how they survived in the midst of so much squalor.

Barefooted black children, with stomachs bloated with hunger, and helpless parents trying to make both ends meet, was a sight that made King cry. He was fiercely determined to bring every black in Marks, Mississippi, to Washington, so that the authorities could be jerked out of their callous slumber.

During this time, he vacillated between lightheadedness and depression, causing worry to his friends and well-wishers. Obsessed with death, he often wondered loudly whether he was doing enough, whether he could do anything more. Rustin was afraid of the psychological deterioration he seemed to be undergoing. He had been receiving threatening calls. Militant black youths had been criticising his non-violent movement and suggesting the authorities could never get the message through non-violence; they scoffed at the idea of a march. The air was thick with hatred and venom.

The day of the downtown march, 22 March 1968, was just round the corner. On 21 March 1968, he was back in Memphis for a strategy session for the march, which, alas, was not to be. The next day, about sixteen inches of snow paralysed Memphis. The scheduled march fell a victim to the vagaries of nature and had to be postponed to Thursday, 28 March 1968.

On 25 March 1968, King appeared before the annual convention of the *Rabbinical Assembly in the Catskill Mountains*, where the rabbis gave a special rendition of *we shall overcome* in Hebrew.

Introducing King to the assembly, his old friend and ally, Rabbi Heschel said, 'Martin Luther King is a voice, a vision and a way. I call upon every Jew to hearken to his voice, to share his vision, to follow in his way. The whole future of America will depend upon the impact and influence of Dr King.'

Although King was very exhausted, he had an interactive session with the audience, wherein he lucidly answered questions ranging from segregation/integration to violence and ghettoes.

Regarding integration, he reiterated:

'We don't want to be integrated out of power, we want to be integrated into power.... We must seek to enrich the ghetto immediately in the sense of improving the housing conditions, improving the schools in the ghetto, improving the economic condition.'

It was in a state of euphoria that King left for New York. The rabbis appeared keen to back the Washington campaign, and that was cause for comfort. But then something happened in New York, which made him feel '*a great sense of loss and remorse*'.

Marion and Dr Arthur Logan were a couple known to the Kings. A top fund-raiser for the SCLC, Marion was of the opinion that the *Poor People's Campaign* was a bad idea and would result in violence. In a memorandum, dated 8 March 1968, which had been sent to each member of the SCLC board, Marion had maintained that the Washington campaign would not move the conscience of Congress and that it should be cancelled.

Sitting in their house in New York, he tried to win them over with a desperate urgency, hurt that he had to convince people who he thought were his friends. Many had tried to warn him against his earlier campaigns. '*If I'd have listened to them, there wouldn't have been a Birmingham, there wouldn't have been a Selma, Montgomery. If I'd have listened to them, we'd not have anything! We'd never have had a movement*', he said.

Despite his vociferous arguments, Marion could not be convinced, and pathetically cheated, King told Bernard Lee, '*Washington DC might be the place he would be clubbed to death, where he could possibly get assassinated.*'

The day of the big March in Memphis, on 28 March 1968, dawned clear. King arrived in Memphis from New York, along with Bernard Lee. At the airport, they were met by Ralph Abernathy, who took them to Clayborn Temple, where a restless crowd of people awaited King.

Interspersed among the peaceful marchers were some black youths who did not subscribe to the ideology of non-violence. King had misgivings. Would they participate in the march? 'No', he was told. But this group of black youth, known as the invaders, happened to be very much a part of the march. As the march started, with King and Abernathy marching at the front, sudden pandemonium broke out. A sixteen-year old boy, Larry Payne, had been shot to death.

The black youth went on a rampage, looting stores and smashing windows. A distraught King beckoned Lawson, '*I will never lead a violent march, so please call it off.*'

'*Disperse; please go to your homes. Please get out*', Rev James Lawson exhorted the marchers. The peaceful ones departed, but the militant youths continued the rampage. Ralph Abernathy and Bernard Lee, horrified at the violent turn that their peaceful march had taken, pushed a reluctant King into a car which Lee drove, after requesting the black woman driver to slide over.

Escorted by a motorcycle cop who led them through a police barricade, King was taken to River Mont Holiday Inn on the banks of the River Mississippi, as the route to Lorraine Hotel, where King wanted to go, was blocked.

In their two-room suite, hunched over with the burden

of grief and guilt, they switched on the television set and images of blood-curdling senseless violence unspooled before their shocked eyes. Black people were clubbed and maced mercilessly, while tear gas drifted across the neighbourhood. There was looting and arson, which stopped only when about four thousand National Guardsmen were ordered into the city by the Governor of Tennessee. State Police riot squads also poured into Memphis.

Lawson told King, 'You must leave. They are going to break up the march and go after you more than anyone.'

On the verge of absolute despair, King indulged in a lot of self-recrimination and just couldn't sleep that night. Horrified that violence would have broken out in a movement that he had lead, and racked with guilt at the brutal killing of Larry Payne by police gunfire, a distraught King told Abernathy: *'It may be that those of us who adhere to non-violence should just step aside and let violent forces run their course, which will be very temporary and very brief, because you can't conduct a violent campaign in this country.'*

His critics had fired salvoes at him earlier on 25 March 1968. Adam Clayton Powell Jr had smugly declared in New York that 'the day of Martin Luther King has come to an end'. With utter disdain, now he called him 'Martin Loser King'.

'None of the precautions he and his aides are taking to keep the capital demonstration peaceful can provide any dependable insurance against another eruption of the kind that rocked Memphis.'

His apprehensions were realised when the newspapers went all out to condemn his methods and the movement. In the

Memphis *Commercial Appeal*, the editorial stated:

> Dr King's pose as a leader of a non-violent movement has been shattered. He now has the entire nation doubting his word when he insists that his April project ... can be peaceful ... furthermore, he wrecked his reputation as a leader, as he took off at high speed when violence occurred, instead of using his persuasive prestige to stop it.'

'A man who hides behind a façade of "non-violence" as he provokes violence', stated *St Louis' Globe Democrat* in a highly accusatory editorial. Equating King with Stokley Carmichael, it reiterated that he 'continues to talk non-violence even as it erupts all about him'.

Was this really the death of his non-violent movement? Were his detractors right when they said that he had outlived his usefulness? But no, he was not going to give up so soon. He had a heavy burden on his shoulders; he had to prove that non-violence was not dead.

A press conference was scheduled for the morning of 29 March 1968 and his mind was in a state of turmoil.

'*Well, Ralph, you can take care of it,*' King said to Abernathy when he told him that three Invaders were waiting to talk to him. In the wash room, while he was getting ready for the conference, he could hear the threesome arguing with Abernathy. What was up? King walked out of the washroom, and tried to soothe frayed nerves and hear their side of the story.

The Invaders – Charles Cabbage, Calvin Taylor and Charles Harrington – conceded that they had instigated the violence, but only because they had been 'snubbed' by the strike leaders and had felt left out and rejected. King tried hard to convince them about the efficacy of non-violence.

At the press conference, he told the assembled people that he was coming back to Memphis as early as 3 April 1968 and no later than 5 April 1968, to lead '*a massive nonviolent demonstration*'.

The media had reported that he had beaten a hasty retreat when the violence had erupted. Denying such an accusation, he maintained that he had not left '*in a hurry*'. He did not want to be associated with *a violent demonstration; hence he had only 'walked' to the car 'agonising over what had happened'*.

He reiterated that the scheduled campaign of 22 April 1968 in Washington would in no way be hindered by the violence.

In a jubilant mood, Ralph Abernathy embraced him warmly in the suite commenting, '*I had never seen the lion in him come forth like that.*'

But the melancholic mood had once again overwhelmed him, and there was a certain desperation in his voice when he muttered to Abernathy, '*Get me out of Memphis as soon as possible. You've got to get me out of Memphis.*'

On Saturday, 30 March 1968, the executive staff of the SCLC had collected at Ebenezer Church in Atlanta. They had a heated discussion regarding King's plan to return to Memphis.

Most of the staff members, including Jesse Jackson and Andrew Bevel, vehemently opposed such a move. They were afraid the SCLC's credibility would be questioned if there was no clear-cut victory in Washington. 'What is our leverage?' they kept asking. 'What is our stick, how do we get out of Washington if we do not win the battle?'

King appeared to have an air of helplessness about him and

Abernathy felt he looked 'very depressed' and 'was back in his shell'.

'I don't even know how to preach people into the Poor Peoples' Campaign', he murmured in a highly demoralised tone.

Walter Fauntroy remarked, 'We've got to go all the way with Martin because he's Martin. I don't care what your reservations are. He's our leader. Let's do what he wants.' However, King continued to be crestfallen and in a highly agitated mood. He asked Abernathy for the keys of his car, as he wanted to go out. To the utter surprise of the staff members, he left the room, with Abernathy close at his heels, worried.

Abernathy wanted to know what was worrying him. King said that he couldn't bear it any longer and that he was going to the country to stay with one of his members. He also assured Abernathy that he would snap out of this melancholic mood, as he had done at the press conference the day before. Returning to the staff meeting, Abernathy told the staff members:

'When the President of our organisation gets troubled, I think the staff ought to come together and quit our bickering and quit our differences.'

Seconding his opinion, Hosea Williams said, 'I agree with you, Mr Vice President, one hundred percent.'

While the others still didn't agree one hundred percent with the proposed second march in Memphis, nonetheless they agreed to march to Washington for the Poor Peoples' Campaign by way of Memphis.

The spirits had again lifted. Hosea Williams started singing and the others also chipped in, singing freedom songs. The moment was opportune for King to be called back. He came back at around 3 pm, still looking forlorn.

In one voice, the staff members agreed that King was right, and that his credibility as a non-violent leader had to be reestablished – they had to return to Memphis to save the *Poor Peoples' Campaign*. King was glad to learn they had now agreed with him, although he still continued to be down in the dumps.

As they were leaving the Church, Jackson called out 'Doc', as though about to say something, while the others looked on. A highly strung King, who had never spoken so angrily to Jackson, retorted, '*Jesse, don't bother me. It may be that you want to carve your own niche in society. Go ahead and carve it. But for God's sake, don't bother me.*'

Putting aside all their doubts and misgivings, all the SCLC members started making preparations for the march, now scheduled for Friday, 5 April 1968. They did not want to take any chances; this time, they worked on the minutest of the details.

Jesse Jackson, Baynard Rustin and others went on a recruitment drive, recruiting churchmen, entertainers, public officials and other labour leaders to join King in Memphis.

On Sunday, 31 March 1968, Hosea Williams, Bevel and others went there to hold workshops on non-violence, to be followed soon by Andrew Young and other staff members.

Another Kennedy to Run for President

In the meantime, something happened, which made King pursue *Poor Peoples' Campaign* with redoubled vigour and a greater determination. On that day, King was in Washington, preaching to an audience, mostly whites, in the Washington Episcopal Cathedral. In the evening, in a nationally televised speech, President Johnson announced a reduction of the bombing in Vietnam, talked of the need for unity in America, the strife that was tearing at the nation's seams. And then, in an explosive Parthian shot, he added:

'I have concluded that I should not permit the presidency to become involved in the partisan divisions that are developing in this political year. Accordingly, I shall not seek, and I will not accept, the nomination of my party for another term as your President.'

In the New Hampshire Democratic primary, Senator Eugene McCarthy of Minnesota had made an impressive showing and Johnson faced almost certain defeat at his hands at the imminent Wisconsin primary.

Robert Kennedy's strength was also growing by leaps and bounds, and Johnson was apprehensive of being challenged for the nomination by him. Vietnam had been his undoing. His political career was doomed. The person who had been elected by an overwhelming majority in 1964, with his vision of a great society, had touched great heights of popularity, but after the Vietnam War, his popularity had nosedived.

President Lyndon Baines Johnson, who had served in all four federal elected offices of the United States – as the Representative from Texas (1937 to 1949), Senator (1949 to 1961), 37th US Vice President (1961 to 1963), and the 36th US President (1963 to 1969) – was now no longer interested in contesting for a second term.

Earlier in 1963, he had won the Presidency by a landslide

61 per cent of the vote, which had been the widest popular margin in the 20th Century at that time.

The visionary who had designed the Great Society legislation, including Civil Rights, who had pushed through the Civil Rights Act through the senate and signed it into law on 2 July 1964, and in 1965, achieved passage of a second Civil Rights Bill – the Voting Rights Act, outlawing discrimination in voting, had withdrawn from the 1968 presidential election race. It was incredible. As this news sunk in, King was dumbfounded. He could not believe his ears.

At the outset, no prominent Democratic candidate was willing to contest against a sitting President of the Democratic Party. But he was challenged by Senator Eugene McCarthy of Minnesota in the New Hampshire primary, who, on 12 March 1968, won 42 per cent of the primary vote to Johnson's 49 per cent, much to the latter's alarm. Robert F Kennedy then entered the race on 16 March 1968.

With the Democratic Party splitting into four factions, it was slipping from President Johnson's hands. The intellectuals and students vehemently opposed the war and supported McCarthy and Robert Kennedy. They also enjoyed the support of Hispanics, Catholics and African Americans. Johnson's popularity painfully plummeted.

On 4 June 1965, Johnson, speaking at the Howard University commencement address, had said that both the government and the nation needed to help achieve goals, to shatter forever not only the barriers of law and public practice, but the walls that bound the condition of many by their skin colour. To dissolve, as best as one can, the ancient enmities of the heart which diminish the holder, divide the great democracy and do wrong – great wrong to the children of God – this very Johnson, who had been telegraphically praised by King for his magnificent speech, who had been hailed as the greatest President the American black had ever had, had suddenly become unpopular.

There was a period which was characterised by a certain warmth in the Johnson-King relations, King believing that the President possessed '*amazing sensitivity to the difficult problems that Negro Americans face in the stride toward freedom*'. Then things started going downhill after a '*little country named Vietnam*' caught Johnson's interest in a big way.

King's denunciation of his Vietnam policies had raised Johnson's heckles, making King a *persona non grata,* hounded by the FBI and criticised by the supporters of war.

Earlier, on 22 November 1963, Lee Harvey Oswald's bullet into President Kennedy had catapulted Johnson into the presidency, but the Vietnam War had pulled him down.

Johnson's withdrawal from the Presidential race was a pleasant surprise for King and his aides.

MEMPHIS, TENNESSEE

ON THE road to the fulfillment of its dream, America had gone off the track. Now with a renewed vigour, the dream had to be realised and the American dilemma had to be resolved with compassion. America had to be brought back on the track. The dreamer had once again started dreaming.

On Wednesday, 3 April 1968, King and his staff members left Atlanta and flew into Memphis. Due to a bomb scare, their flight was delayed, all bags were checked and the plane was guarded and protected which King found *ridiculous*. In the plane, Ralph Abernathy was pleased to find him in a pleasant mood, talking about myriad topics.

Several black leaders greeted King's group at the gate. Four detectives from the Memphis police department, and a bunch of cameramen and journalists also waited for him. In view of the threats to his life, he was whisked away to Lorraine Hotel at 405, Mulberry Street Rock Road, where he checked into Room 306 along with Abernathy.

[Owned by a black businessman, Walter Bailey, and named partly after his wife, Loree, and partly as homage to Nat 'King'

Cole's song *Sweet Lorraine,* the hotel was converted into the national Civil Rights Museum in 1991.]

Built in 1925 and originally called the Windsor Hotel, King had savoured many a home-cooked meal here prior to his last and fateful visit. King and his '*best friend*' Ralph Abernathy had stayed so often in Room 306, that it was referred to as *the King Abernathy suite* – this time, alas, King checked-in for the last time.

Despite King's disapproval, two detectives set up a surveillance post at a fire station in the vicinity, keeping the Lorraine Motel under a constant observation from the fire station from behind a papered-up window. During the day, King squeezed-in many conferences and meetings about the imminent march.

Bayard Rustin and others advised him to postpone the march to Monday, 8 April 1968, which would provide enough time for different groups to come to Memphis, and also give them ample time for making further preparations to ensure the march would be non-violent.

Meanwhile, frantic efforts were in full swing to nip the movement in the bud, what the detractors thought was an evil. With this aim, Mayor Loeb applied to the federal district court for an injunction against the proposed march, which was issued in the afternoon. But this failed to dishearten King or the SCLC lawyers. While King vowed to lead the march, telling reporters that '*we are not going to be stopped by mace or injunctions*', SCLCS legal counsel, Chauncey Eskridge, planned to challenge the injunction in the federal courthouse the next day.

On the afternoon of 3 April 1968, when the sky was overcast with menacing looking clouds, King's heart and mind were in turmoil. Thunder cracked and lightning flashed outside, but on King's mental horizon, there were no flashes of light. His erratic mood had again swung towards depression and dark thoughts. Had he lost his appeal? Was non-violence dead? Racked by apprehensions and misgivings, he decided not to go to Mason Temple where he was scheduled to address a rally. What if there was a meager turnout, wouldn't that be an implication that Martin Luther King Jr was no longer a force to reckon with? And if he had lost his charisma, his touch?

He asked a reluctant Abernathy to go to Mason Temple and speak in his place. When Abernathy reached the Temple, he was pleasantly surprised to find that nearly two thousand people had braved the torrential rains to listen to their leader, Martin Luther King Jr However, with a sense of utter disappointment, they were to realise King had not come.

An utterly exhausted and apprehensive King was trying to relax in bed. Around 8.30 pm, his phone rang and Abernathy tried to cajole him to come over to Mason Temple, as the enthusiastic crowd was eagerly waiting to hear him.

'Come on, Ralph. Can't you talk to them? Won't they listen to you?' King insisted.

But Abernathy was unwilling to listen. He pleaded, 'I really think you should come down. The people want to hear you, not me. This is your crowd.'

King was left with no choice. Although demoralised, and totally tired, he finally decided to go. He dressed up and went out in a torrential rain, which was lashing out with vengeance. As he climbed the dais, he received a rousing welcome while the rain provided the background music – beating and lashing. Shrugging away the pangs of apprehension, King's eyes swept across the packed hall.

'*Ralph Abernathy is the best friend that I have in the world,*' he said after Abernathy had introduced him. Then, with a spontaneous passion, King spoke, while the enthusiastic people who had been clamoring for their eloquent leader, hung on to every word that he uttered, interjecting with '*Go ahead! Go ahead!*', '*Yeah, Oh yes, yes doctor*', and '*Yes, Sir, go ahead, Amen!*' And their leader went ahead, taking the thunderous applause in his stride, taking the audience along with him on his mental flight from Egypt … through the wilderness on toward the Promised Land.

'*And I would see Plato, Aristotle, Socrates, Euripides and Aristophanes assembled around the Parthenon, as they discussed the great and eternal issues of reality.*' The heydays of the Roman Empire, the *Renaissance* and the *Reformation*, Abraham Lincoln signing the *Emancipation Proclamation* in 1863 and Franklin Roosevelt signing the *New Deal* in the 1930s, grappling with the problems of the bankruptcy of his nation.

Of late, death had stalked him relentlessly, yet King's words did not lack optimism when he said:

> *And I'm happy that he's allowed me to be in Memphis. I can remember when Negroes were just going around, as Ralph has said, scratching where they didn't itch, and laughing when they*

were not tickled. But that day is all over. We mean business now, and we are determined to gain our rightful place in God's world. We are saying that we are God's children. And that we don't have to live like we are forced to live.

Something is happening in our world. The masses of people are rising up. And wherever they are assembled today, the cry is always the same – "We want to be free."

The press very seldom got around to mentioning the fact that one thousand, three hundred sanitation workers were on strike, and that Memphis is not being fair to them.... Now we're going to march again, and we've got to march again and force everybody to see that there are thirteen hundred of God's children here suffering, sometimes going hungry, going through dark and dreary nights.... For when people get caught up with that which is right and they are willing to sacrifice for it, there is no stopping point short of victory.

He reiterated that they were not going to let any injunction deter them.

'All we say to America is: "Be true to what you said on paper." If I lived in China or even Russia, or may be any totalitarian country, may be I could understand the denial of certain basic first amendment privileges. Somewhere, I read that the greatness of America is the right to protest for right... we aren't going to let any injunction turn us around, we are going on.'

Although, there was an underlying note of despair in his sermon that day, the thought of death always being there, yet he was optimistic enough to proclaim that one day his dream of *'the brotherhood of man will become a reality ... and with this faith, I will go out and carve a tunnel of hope from a mountain of despair....'*

The person, who had climbed the dais with a weary spirit, mopping his forehead and thinking loudly, had slowly yanked away his somber mood and, towards the end of his speech, had managed to lift himself out of the dumps.

Voicing a passionate yearning, going down the meandering lanes and by-lanes of memory, reminiscing about being stabbed ten years back, the sit-ins and freedom rides, his *I have a dream* speech, his various movements in Albany, Birmingham, Selma and now Memphis, his voice had become increasingly electrifying and, towards the end of his speech, he had spoken the prophetic words, which now reverberate in history:

> *'I've seen the Promised Land. I may not get there with you but I want you to know tonight, that we, as a people, will get to the Promised Land.'*

Although King was overwhelmed with apprehension before the sermon, yet the presence of an audience of about two thousand people, who had come despite the storm warning and were very keen to listen to him, had lifted his sagging spirits. The sermon was like a therapeutic auto-suggestion, which had injected a new hope in him, banishing the earlier misgivings and anxiety.

There was a dramatic change in the King who had returned to Lorraine Hotel that rainy night. Gone were the earlier dark and dismal thoughts and, in a happy frame of mind, he started working on a sermon for the following Sunday.

It was as if, by inspiring and stimulating the people into believing that, despite the '*difficult days ahead, I will go out and carve a tunnel of hope from a mountain of despair …*', he had inspired and stimulated himself.

His brother AD King arrived from Louisville after midnight and King was with him until the wee hours of the morning.

THE LAST MOMENTS

IT WAS with the stirrings of a new dawn, which, alas, would be King's last! He turned in after 4 am, on 4 April 1968.

Later, around mid-morning, Ralph Abernathy tried to nudge him into wakefulness.

'Come on, it's time to get up.'

'Yes', King mumbled in a voice groggy with sleep, but made no move to get up.

Abernathy, known for his tremendous sense of humour, rejoined: 'You know, we can't get this non-violent revolution in bed.'

'I'm never going to get the farmer out of you', King remarked to his friend, who was born on his farmer father's 500-acre farm in Linden, Alabama, about 42 years back.

The new day seemed to have infused a new zest into King and he was rearing to go headlong into the activities lined up for the day. He shaved and showered, and asked Abernathy to take some important notes and make some phone calls regarding the day's activities.

Later, he had a meeting with his executive staff, discussing the legalities and logistics of the forthcoming Memphis march. They also decided to postpone the march until the following Monday, 8 April 1968. Eskridge was at the federal courthouse trying to get the temporary injunction against the march lifted, and Andrew Young went there to give him this news.

Meanwhile, King and his staff conferred with a group of Invaders and some members of the black organising project, a group of militant students. King wondered whether they could be employed as march marshals, and whether they could give school kids lessons in non-violence. Abernathy felt that they were not shabby-looking, but appeared quite intelligent.

The boys agreed to talk to the school kids, though maintaining emphatically that they could not totally rule out violence. Moreover, they demanded four to five cars to move around. King did not yield to their demands but later was appalled to find that four Invaders had been put on the SCLC's staff and payroll.

'*Advocates of violence could definitely not be tolerated on the staff*', King told his aides, who were abashed. They informed the youth likewise, who checked out of the motel.

Due to the violence on 28 March 1968, King wanted to prove that non-violence was not dead, and that they could still carry out a non-violent march in Washington. Violence was something which he abhorred. His moral tenacity, reminiscent of a frail figure, whom Winston Churchill had called the '*half-naked fakir*', prodded him on, only to fall a victim to something which he deplored with all he heart.

It was the time for lunch now.

They ordered one of their favourite dishes – catfish and salad

– to be brought to Room 306, but to Abernathy's irritation, the waitress brought the catfish in one plate. Dissuading Abernathy from sending the waitress back for another plate, King offered to eat from the same plate. They found the catfish delicious.

After lunch, Abernathy decided to give in to the luxury of forty winks, while King went to his brother AD's room, from where they called their mother, who was delighted to hear that the two brothers were together.

At 4 pm, King asked Abernathy to come over to AD's room, where they indulged in a lot of light-hearted chatter. King even told Abernathy about his telephone call to his mother, and how happy she was to learn the brothers were together.

Not very fond of broccoli, asparagus and cauliflower, King was very keen to know about the menu for the dinner at Rev Samuel Kyles home.

'Lots of soul food, chitterlings, black-eyed peas, greens and pig's feet and also prime rib roast,' Abernathy repeated to King what Mrs Kyles had said to him over the phone. King was delighted, he started looking forward to dinner with greater zest.

'*We're home free*,' Chauncey Eskridge yelled storming into the room, along with Andrew Young, their faces jubilant. They had been in the court the entire day fighting an injunction, preventing the SCLC from launching another march, the apprehension being that more violence would be triggered, which would be 'worse than Watts or Detroit'.

At the court, Andrew Young and Lawson had brilliantly pleaded their case, giving a magnificent philosophical presentation, arguing that a non-violent march would not trigger violence but, on the contrary, it would unify the black community preventing Detroit-like violence.

So impressed was the judge that he ruled in their favour, allowing the march to take place, provided they marched six abreast with marshals at every four ranks.

It was now 5 pm, and they had to get ready for the dinner. King and Abernathy left AD's room and returned to Room 306. Once again, King shaved and applied *Aramis* aftershave face lotion, while all the time chatting with Abernathy.

Abernathy told him that he wouldn't be able to attend the initial march in Washington because its timing clashed with his other preoccupation – that of conducting a revival in his church in Atlanta. But King would have none of it, as he said:

'*…tell them, that you have a greater revival, a revival to revive the soul of this nation and cause America to feed the hungry, to have concern for those who are downtrodden and disinherited…*'

Ultimately, Abernathy yielded to his affectionate insistence.

'Are you ready?' he asked Abernathy.

'Wait just a minute, let me put on some aftershave lotion,' Abernathy replied.

[Later, he recalled that had it not been for *Aramis* aftershave lotion, he would also have been in the line of fire.]

'*Ok, I'll be standing out here on the balcony*,' King remarked and stepped out of Room 306, along with Rev Kyles. Both stood leaning against the iron-railing along the balcony, and his eyes fell on Jesse Jackson, his 27-year old aide, wearing a brown turtleneck overbrown slacks, standing in the parking lot with Ben Branch.

Andrew Young was bantering with Bernard Lee and Hosea Williams, and Rev James Orange and James Bevel were playfully wrestling, absolutely relaxed after spending the entire day at Clayburn Temple church organising non-violent workshops for the youth.

'Don't let him hurt you,' King said to Rev Bevel. Rev Orange had picked up Bevel and was holding him aloft.

'We're on the way to Rev Kyles' home for dinner, and you don't have a tie on,' King remarked to Jackson.

Kyles had moved away from the balcony by that time and was on his way down the stairs and Martin stood there alone, looking down on his friends, bantering with them.

'Doc, the prerequisite for eating is an appetite, not a tie,' Jackson countered with a smile.

'*Ben, be sure to play my favourite song tonight – Precious Lord*,' King then said gesturing to Ben Branch, the leader of a band Jackson had brought to Memphis.

'You know it's cool, and you've had a cold. You better go back and get your topcoat,' Andrew Young suggested.

'*Do I really need a coat?*' King asked.

Solomon Jones also asked him to get his topcoat at which King remarked, '*Solomon, you really know how to take good care of me.*' Then he asked Abernathy to get his top-coat for him.

In Room 306, Abernathy stood before the mirror, and poured some cologne into his hands. He had hardly lifted the hands to his face, when he heard what he thought sounded like a firecracker. He dashed towards the door, and a cold chill ran up his spine as he saw King lying on the balcony floor with his feet protruding through the balcony railing, his hands rigid at his throat, his dream cut short.

In utter horror, Abernathy stumbled forward and, in doing

so, stepped over his seriously wounded friend. '*Oh my God, Martin's been shot,*' an anguished cry wrenched from his heart.

In the last hour alive, King had just had a pillow fight with his friend in his motel room, talked of gospel music, soul food, neckties and the high price of righteousness.

On learning what had happened, an utterly devastated Kyles also dashed to Room 306 to call an ambulance. But the operator, the motel owner Walter Bailey's wife, was nowhere to be seen. In impotent sorrow, he repeatedly hit his head against the wall.

Mrs Lorree Catherine Bailey, Kyles later found out, had gone down to the parking lot. What she saw there was so traumatic for her that she collapsed with a heart attack and succumbed to it five days later.

I'm sorry, but we've lost him

'*I'm sorry, but we've lost him. It's all over,*' the head physician at St Joseph's hospital finally said to Ralph Abernathy and Bernard Lee. There had been massive damage to the brain due to lack of

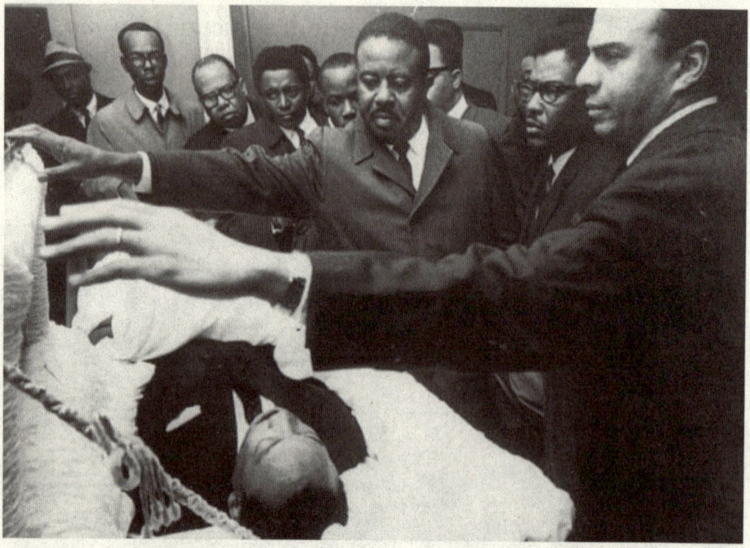

oxygen. The doctors said even if he would have lived, he would have been a vegetable – paralysed from his neck downwards.

The bullet, a metal jacketed 30-60, had penetrated through his neck, damaging vital arteries and fracturing the spine in many places.

Ralph Abernathy – whom he had called '*the best friend that I have in the world*' just a day back, and whom he had talked out with his words '*we've been together so far and there is no need for us to separate now*' just over an hour ago when Abernathy had said he couldn't attend the initial march to Washington – was being told by the doctor that it was all over.

Abernathy's best friend now lay lifeless and dreamless on the table, while the many moments that they had spent together – right from the Montgomery bus boycott to the Memphis sanitation workers strike, the preparation for the *Poor People's Campaign* – everything unspooled before his eyes.

For this right hand man of King, everything appeared wrong and absolutely topsy-turvy. They had almost been like conjoined Siamese twins, preaching, marching, negotiating together and, on many an occasion, being jailed together. The fears, frustrations, doubts, and misgivings and their tenacity in the face of it all, came before his eyes in one cascading flash.

It was in Montgomery in 1954, that King had struck a friendship with the 29-year old short, stocky, charming man with whom he was to share fourteen years of fun, frolic, laughter and tears. Four years older than King, they had complemented each other, Abernathy becoming his alter-ego, spending many moments on the roads together, swaying and prancing arm-in-arm during parties, singing off-key songs, much to the embarrassed delight of their spouses.

Their sense of humor was so infectious that they could have their friends in splits, King with his gentle humor and gift of the repartee and Abernathy with his crude and rough humour.

When Abernathy's home and church had been bombed in the pre-dawn hours of 10 January 1957 in Montgomery, King and Abernathy had been asleep in the King home in Atlanta. An urgent phone call from Juanita Abernathy had informed them about the bombing and four other explosions in the vicinity. Both had then prayed together for endurance and strength.

Now Abernathy was alone, not having the strength to carry on. In a daze, he and Barnard Lee collected his personal effects from his coat and trouser pocket and went into a small anteroom where Andrew Young sat with his head buried in his hands – a picture of absolute desolation. From an adjoining room, Chauncey Eskridge walked into the anteroom, and Abernathy blurted out: 'Now Martin is gone from us. Now we are alone.'

Chauncey Eskridge told him that Abernathy was their leader now, and added, 'We are going to take you in front of the TV cameras and then we'll go to the airport and wait for Coretta.'

[While travelling by car towards Selma, and heading along Highway 80 – also known as the Jefferson Davis Highway – on 2 January 1965, an apprehensive King, airing his views about the rampant violence, had said to Abernathy: '*Ralph, I thought I would have been assassinated in Mississippi but it did not happen, so it will probably come to me over here in Selma. So I want to fix it so that you will automatically become my successor without having to have a board meeting or anything.*']

Despite King's persistence, Abernathy had insisted that he did not want the SCLC presidency. But now at this sudden and sad turn of events, the SCLC presidency was staring him in the face.

They looked at each other in mute horror, reeling under their colossal loss, and fell into each others arms weeping together. Abernathy said a prayer for his departed friend and then Chauncey Eskridge and Andrew Young propelled him out of the door where the television cameramen and reporters were waiting.

Abernathy spoke in a daze. Then he, along with Bernard Lee, Eskridge and Young, climbed into a waiting car to pick up Coretta from the airport. As soon as the news reached Coretta, she headed for the airport along with Mayor Allen and his spouse. But on hearing that he had succumbed to his wounds, an utterly shaken Coretta decided to go home to her children.

From St Joseph's Hospital, King's body was taken to John Gaston Hospital's Memphis Morgue, where the medical examiner wanted Abernathy to identify the man in the next room.

Choking with emotion 'the best friend' that King had in the world, touched his lifeless friend on the cheek and blurting out, 'Yes, that's him,' and dashed out of the morgue.

Although Abernathy had imagined the inevitable, he had never thought that he would be left alone. Later, like a left-behind twin, he suffered from protracted illness, often wondering why they could not have gone together.

'I thought that somebody would put a bomb in the car. We were always riding together. And it would go off and we would just be killed together. And when it happened, we were together, and the only thing that saved me was Aramis cologne. I would have been in the line of fire, I guess,' he later said.

The man – who had felt the shadow of his own death, lurking in corners, lying in ambush, and had almost foretold it in the prophetic finale of his last sermon – was now eerily quiet, so were the streets around Lorraine Motel, as utterly dazed people milled around in the dark.

In his monogrammed briefcase in Room 306, besides the usual paraphernalia – shaving crème, pajamas, brush – there was also his book *Strength to Love.* Yes, he had immense strength to love, preaching it to all, writing about the redemptive power of love, even trying to turn the *Black Power* protagonists to his way of thinking, nursing no rancor against Izola Curry, the woman who had tried to stab him. He carried no ill will even against diehard racists like Bull Connor.

In September 1962, while he was delivering an impassioned address at the SCLC's convention in Birmingham, a heavily-built white youth sitting in the audience had lunged at him and punched him on his nose. With the intervention of the police and some SCLC delegates, the youth, a self-styled Nazi, was mollified, but King had insisted that he should be permitted to sit among the audience again.

After the meeting, King had said '*I'm not interested in pressing charges. I'm interested in changing the kind of system that produces this kind of man.*'

At Atlanta, Coretta was appalled to hear that King had allowed the boy to stay in the audience. 'Suppose he had a knife or a gun?' she had asked.

'*Well, if he had, he would have used it before,*' was King's answer.

As Benjamin E Mays said in his final eulogy: This man had no bitterness in his heart, no rancor in his soul, no revenge in his mind, and he went up and down the length and breadth of this world, preaching non-violence and the redemptive power of love.

In Ebenezer Church, his parents were stunned, as they heard the terrible news over the radio. The grief-stricken twosome clung to each other, as silent tears fell down their cheeks. In April 1968, when King had gone to Memphis, his parents had been very tense. In his autobiography, *Daddy King: An Autobiography* [1980, Beacon Press, 2017], his father, Daddy King wrote:

> The tension of those months took a heavy toll on Bunch who was always aware of the pressure both the boys were under in their daily lives. The sound of a telephone, our doorbell ringing, any call that brought with it some news, edged up on us like a series of loud, sudden alarms.
>
> Suddenly in a few seconds of radio time, it was all over.
>
> My first son, whose birth had brought me such joy that I jumped up in the hall outside the room where he was born and touched the ceiling – the child, the scholar, the preacher all were gone.

THE SUN DISAPPEARS BELOW THE HORIZON

JUST FOUR years ago, his son had won the Nobel Peace Prize and King Sr had travelled with him to accept this honour. In his autobiography, he wrote: 'As ML stood receiving the Nobel Prize, and the tears just streamed down my face, I gave thanks that out of that tiny Georgia town I'd been spared to see this and so much else.'

Those were tears of joy at so stupendous an achievement and now the tears that streamed down his face told a different story – a story of utter loss, the loss of a sixty-nine year old father and a sixty-four year old mother of their thirty-nine year old son.

Overwhelmed by the cascading assault of memories of their son – the boy ML playing baseball, flying kites and model airplanes, pedaling a bicycle in the serene neighbourhood of Auburn Avenue, Atlanta, slipping down banisters, listening to Biblical stories from Mama Dear – their world suddenly seemed to have collapsed around them. The '*talkative chap*' had fallen silent.

The sun had disappeared below the horizon and darkness

pervaded. At this national disaster, the nation had gone berserk with grief. The great warrior, the indefatigable crusader, who, despite adverse criticism, had walked on, waging an unending war against the centennial injustice, laughing away the epithets hurled at him, would now walk no more.

For some, he was 'Martin Loser King'; for some others 'a traitor to his cause'; and for still others, he was 'a misguided Moses'. There was no dearth of allegations flung at him. Accused of 'criminal disobedience', he was at the receiving end of many a hate-campaign. Serious charges of embezzlement, of sexual misconduct, of hobnobbing with the communists, were levelled against him, and many Confederationists wished him dead.

No matter what he was called, no matter what he was accused of, he remained Martin to the last day, the same compassionate, sensitive soul, whose heart bled at the injustice all around, often feeling guilty that he had not been born into poverty. Martin, a vulnerable man with his human frailties, was not a flawless saint! Whatever the doubts he was plagued with, howsoever heavy the burden he was weighed under, he was determined to make the world a better place to live in.

Hence, despite his friends' advice to take a break, he plunged forth at a frenetic pace, time and again racked by apprehensions, but reiterating a person is not fit to live if he has not found a cause to die for. And indeed he died for a cause – a cause very dear to his heart, a cause which permeated his very being. While death stalked him, he walked on, and he talked on – walked on towards the Promised Land. But midway, he was embraced by redemptive death. He talked on about his commitment to a moral ideal. But midway, the voice got throttled. But the ideal lived on and breathed on, in his followers and friends.

Like the Good Samaritan in the Old Testament, King had stopped in Memphis to help someone – the sanitation workers. With a kind of dangerous unselfishness, he had managed to project the *I* into the *thou.* And to be concerned about his brethren – the sanitation workers – he had lost his life.

The sanitation workers universally acknowledged their great debt to this good Samaritan, who hammered away relentlessly with his non-violent hammer, and demanded dignity for the sanitation workers, who hauled garbage, stank, lived in absolute poverty, suffered from high blood pressure, diabetes, anemia and did not have the wherewithal to get themselves treated.

King's coming to Memphis injected some energy in the demoralised community, who thought that he was an emissary from God.

Although King died fighting for the sanitation workers, he did not die in vain. He was able to win for them the right to be treated like humans, and prod the conscience of a nation indifferent to the pleas and cries of those human beings who had been deprived of dignity.

The strike became a local movement coalescing in the *Poor People's Campaign.*

King had said, *'The question is not "if I stop to help this man in need what will happen to me". The question is "If I do not stop to help the sanitation workers what will happen to them."'*

So, King had risen with a *'greater readiness, with a greater determination'* to make America what it ought to be… a better nation.

Robert F Kennedy arrived by plane at Indianapolis, where he was informed of King's death.

Breaking this tragic news to a large gathering of African Americans he said:

> *Martin Luther King dedicated his life to love and to justice between fellow human beings. He died in the cause of that effort...*
>
> *For those of you who are black – considering the evidence evidently is that there where white people who were responsible – you can be filled with bitterness, and with hatred, and a desire for revenge.*
>
> *We can move in that direction as a country, in greater polarisation – black people amongst blacks, and white amongst whites, filled with hatred toward one another, or we can make an effort, as Martin Luther King did, to understand and to comprehend, and replace that violence that stain of blood shed that has spread across our land, with an effort to understand, compassion and love.*
>
> *My favourite poet was Aeschylus. He once wrote, even in our sleep, pain which cannot forget falls drop by drop upon the heart, until, in our own despair, against our will comes wisdom through the awful grace of God.*
>
> *What we need in the United States is not division; what we need in the United States is not hatred; what we need in the United States is not violence or lawlessness, but love and wisdom, and compassion toward one another, and a feeling of justice towards those who still suffer within our country, whether they be white or they be black.*
>
> *Let us dedicate ourselves to what the Greeks wrote so many years ago: to tame the savageness of man and to make gentle the life of this world.*

A fuming Stokley Carmichael, the proponent of *Black Power*, with whom King had had many a heated discussion cried, '*When white America killed Dr King, she declared war on us.*' He exhorted the blacks to get their guns. Propounding the *Black Power* ideology, he said, 'We have to be able to smash any political machine in the country that's oppressing us and bring it to its knees.'

President Johnson, who postponed a trip to Hawaii for peace talks on Vietnam, was 'shocked and saddened', pleading with every citizen to reject the blind violence that had taken King's life, a person who lived by non-violence.

More than hundred US cities witnessed riots in the wake of Martin Luther King's death. In Memphis, about four thousand members of the National Guard were drafted, and a dusk-to-dawn curfew was clamped. The worst affected cities were Chicago, Baltimore and Washington DC.

A 28-block stretch of West Madison Street in the black ghetto on the west side in Chicago was destroyed. The corridor – between Roosevelt Road on the south and Chicago Avenue on the north – was witness to widespread arson and looting. It was as if a wave of madness had seized Chicago. A health clinic in Chicago which provided free healthcare to children and infants was also set ablaze.

An aerial view of Washington showed a smoke-sheathed capital, looking as though it were bombed. Some rabid racists were secretly delighted that the man, who had shamed them into feeling guilty, had been assassinated.

There was an outpouring of grief from all over the world. The Foreign Minister of Japan, Takeo Niki, said that his country was 'gravely concerned'.

Reverend Trevor Huddleston of Tanzania, who had been expelled from South Africa for daring to raise his voice against apartheid, said that King's death was the greatest single tragedy since Gandhi's death.

In Britain and France, the newspapers condemned the racism and violence rampant in America. Both parties in the English House of Commons passed resolutions expressing their sense of outrage.

All over the world, the news of King's death plunged the people into grief, dominating the radio, press and the television. There were special editions of newspapers about King in South Africa. The '*sad and inhumane killing*' was mourned by the officials in Lagos, Nigeria, and a portrait of King draped in black crepe was hung outside the front door of the US Embassy. Both houses of parliament in West Germany stood in silent tribute and a march of about a thousand Germans and Americans was led by Mayor Klaus Schutz through West Berlin to John F Kennedy Square.

Robert Kennedy who had become increasingly close to King in the last years of his life, raising the heckles of President Johnson, chartered an Electra Jet to bring King's body from Memphis to Atlanta, accompanied by Coretta and AD.

Absolutely dazed mourners of all races paid their tributes to King. The devastated parents came along with Coretta and the four children.

Despite his exhortation '*I don't want a long funeral*', this visionary, this dreamer, this towering hero, this charismatic figure, this philosopher, was destined to get a long funeral.

From the *Montgomery Bus boycott* (1955-1956) to the *Freedom Rides* (1960-61), *Albany Movement* (1961-62) to Birmingham and the *March on Washington* (1963), to Alabama and St Augustine (1963-64), then to Selma (1965), followed by *Chicago* and the *War on Slums* (1965-1966), then to the *Meredith March* (1966), and finally to the *Poor People's Campaign* and *Memphis* (1967), this indefatigable and unrelenting non-violent warrior had marched and fought for thirteen years. And now, he was tired, very tired, so tired that even his father's beseeching tones, '*Open your eyes, Martin. Answer me, ML*' failed to wake him up.

Sobbing uncontrollably, Daddy King could now touch only the mortal remains of his son, as he lay lifeless and wordless in the casket. '*He never hated anybody, he never hated anybody*', the distraught father muttered as he collapsed, overwhelmed by sobs.

April 9, 1968, Atlanta

The sun poured its wrath, perhaps angry at the unfairness and injustice of it all that a man in the prime of youth – brimming with vigor, dreaming big dreams for his brethren – should have been so cruelly snatched from the midst of the people, who had been told just a few days back, that they would definitely get to the Promised Land. How would they get to the Promised Land now, with their leader gone?

Two funeral services were held for King – one was at Ebenezer Baptist Church, where both father and son had served as pastors for many years. Here, the attendance was limited to friends, family members of the congregation and other important guests, and the other at Morehouse College, King's *alma mater*.

Such a massive crowd had turned up outside the Church, that family and friends had a tough time trying to get in.

More than sixty thousand people attended his funeral service, which included four presidential contenders – Senator Robert Kennedy, Senator Eugene McCarthy, Vice President Hubert Humphrey, and Richard Nixon. Besides, there were black entertainers. President Johnson had been dissuaded from attending.

Harry Belafonte and his wife, Diana Ross, as also Thurgod Marshall, Sammy Davis and Mahalia Jackson were there. So were Andrew Young, Hosea Williams, Bernard Lee and Stokley Carmichael. Accompanied by six guards, Jacqueline Kennedy, attired in a black silk mourning dress, created quite a stir.

Mourners lined the streets waiting for the funeral procession to pass their way; everything moving before their eyes in a surreal haze. People stood everywhere, craning their necks trying to catch a glimpse of the casket, some even stood on motorbikes, cars and jeeps.

This spokesman of the blacks could now no longer speak.

The famous and eloquent baritone had been stilled. The words that he had vowed to cultivate from a very early age had been throttled '*You just wait and see, when I grow up I'm going to get me some big words*,' he had promised his parents.

Gladstone Lewis Chandlers' expert prodding at Morehouse College had helped him in withdrawing '*rich dividends*' and mesmerising his audience. But now these words would no longer throb, captivate or mesmerise with passion. They were as lifeless as the body that lay in the African mahogany coffin with its cross of flowers.

While King's family sat bowed down under the weight of their colossal grief, Abernathy spoke: '*We gather here this morning in one of the darkest hours in the history of the black people of this nation.*' However, as Ralph Abernathy believed, his words would never die, 'they will live in our minds and our hearts and in the souls of black men and white men, brown men and yellow men as long as time shall last.'

Many a time, his powerful baritone had quoted the old slave spiritual:

Free at Last, Free at Last
Thank God Almighty
I'm Free at Last.

Now these words were etched on his crypt.

Finally, the marchers reached Morehouse College, where he had enrolled at an exceptionally young age of 15, and where he blossomed under intellectual giants like Walter Chivers, Gladstone Lewis Chandler, George D Kelsey, and the gracefully tall, articulate Benjamin Elijah Mays, who King called his '*spiritual mentor*' and '*intellectual father*'.

It was under his hypnotic spell that, at the age of seventeen, after initial misgivings, he had realised that the ministry was his true calling, and like his father and maternal grandfather had decided to become a Baptist minister.

Now this outstanding teacher, mentor, scholar, preacher, a giant in the Christian ministry, the seventy-year old President Emeritus of Morehouse College, with a heavy heart, delivered his last eulogy for a person who was like a son:

> So close and precious was he to me.
>
> God called the grandson of a slave on his father's side, and the grandson of a man born during the civil war, on his mother's side, and said to him. Martin Luther, speak to America about war and peace, about social justice and racial discrimination; about its obligation to the poor; and about non-violence as a way of perfecting social change in a world of brutality and war.
>
> It was my desire that if I predeceased Dr King, he would pay tribute to me on my final day. It was his wish that if he predeceased me, I would deliver the eulogy at his funeral. Fate has decreed that I eulogise him. I wish it might have been otherwise.
>
> He died striving to desegregate and integrate America to the end that this great nation of ours, born in revolution and blood, conceived in liberty and dedicated in the proposition that all men are created free and equal, will truly become the lighthouse of freedom where none will be denied because his skin is black and none favoured because his eyes are blue; where the poorest – the garbage collectors – will have bread enough and to spare; where no one will be poorly housed …
>
> As Mahatma Gandhi challenged the British Empire without a sword and won, Martin Luther King Jr challenged the interracial wrongs of his country without a gun.… But Martin Luther faced the dogs, the police, jail, heavy criticism and finally death; and he never carried a gun, not even a knife to defend himself. He had only his faith in a just God to rely on;… the faith that Browning writes about

> when he says: "One who never turned his back but marched breast forward; Never doubted clouds would break; Never dreamed, though right were worsted, wrong would triumph; Held we fall to rise, are baffled to fight better; sleep to wake." He was supra-race, supra-nation, supra-denomination, supra-class and supra-culture. He belonged to the world and to mankind. Now he belongs to posterity....
>
> Too bad, you say, that Martin Luther King Jr died so young. I feel that way too. But, as I have said many times before, it isn't how long one lives, but how well; it's what one accomplishes for mankind that matters. Jesus died at 33; Joan of Arc at 19; Byron and Burns at 36, Keats at 25; Marlow at 29; Shelley at 30; Dunbar before 35; John Fitzgerald Kennedy at 46; William Rainey Harper at 49; and Martin Luther King Jr at 39.

Then, with heavy hearts, leaden feet and limpid eyes, the mourners headed towards South View Cemetery with the coffin of their hero. There was spring in the air, with luxuriant greenery all around, but a chilly winter seemed to have settled in their hearts. Here his grandparents lay peacefully in eternal sleep.

The thirty-nine-year-old grandson was buried next to his '*mama*', Grandmother Williams, whose sudden death, on another spring day on 18 May 1941, had so devastated the twelve-year-old, that he had tried to leap from the window of their house, wondering how he could survive without the one who loved him so much.

The indefatigable crusader, who, in the last years of his life, had been lost in the ebb and flow of a turbulent sea, restless, melancholic, and also euphoric, was finally free. Free of his dreams and visions for his brethren; and also the nightmares that had stalked him in his later years.

Strongly believing like Thoreau, that even a minority of '*one honest man*' could set in motion a moral revolution, King had set about launching a '*moral revolution*'. This '*one honest man*' galvanised an entire community into action, jerked them out of their centennial slumber, and prodded them to march on towards freedom. The images of poor and unlettered folks, with tired feet and rested souls marching on during the Montgomery bus boycott, still shines bright from the sepia-tinted pages of history.

Many images flash before one's eyes:

- King flashing the victory sign in St Augustine, Florida, after hearing of the passage of the Civil Rights Bill on 19 June 1964.
- President Johnson shaking hands with King on 3 July 1964 in Washington DC, and handing him a pen during the signing of the Civil Rights Bill in the White House; and
- King receiving the Nobel Peace Prize from Gunnar Jahn, the Chairman of the Nobel Peace Prize Committee in Oslo, Norway, on 10 December 1964.

In the Presidential speech he was applauded as:

> 'A man who has never abandoned his faith in the unarmed struggle he is waging, who has suffered for his faith, who has been imprisoned on many occasions, whose home has been subjected to bomb attacks, whose life and the lives of his family have been threatened, and who nevertheless has never faltered.

These images rise above the images of:

- Steel-helmeted policemen swinging nightsticks in an effort to break up street gatherings;

- Images of National Guard troops with upthrust bayonets, surrounding integrationists as they made a peaceful attempt to challenge the no-demonstration edict of the military commander in Cambridge, Maryland, on 13 May 1964;
- King sitting in a police car in the back seat with a police dog after testifying before a grand jury investigating racial unrest in the city on 12 June 1964;
- JB Stone, a diehard segregationist from Atlanta, Georgia, holding a Confederate flag, while addressing a whole gathering of whites at a slave market in St Augustine, Florida, on 13 June 1964, while a placard in the background proclaimed: '*Kill Civil Rights Bill.*'

At the twice-weekly mass meetings in Montgomery, King would talk about non-violence, emphasising, that, '*to meet hate with retaliatory violence would do nothing but intensify the existence of evil in the universe. Hate begets hate, violence begets violence, toughness begets greater toughness.*'

The vicious power which came from fire hoses, night sticks, bayonets, cow prods, dogs, curses evanesced before the sublime power of a voice fortified by the power of love.

Through the vistas of time, that powerful, impassioned baritone, cruelly stilled on 4 April 1968, still exhorts us, encourages us, prods and cajoles us – a voice so mesmerising that the churchwomen would often say that when he spoke they could see the wings of angels flying around his head – a voice infused with such an incredible poetic majesty that even the unlettered were inspired – a voice which still goads us on to new dreams, new visions, new hopes.

Epilogue

On a cold, cloudy January day of the year 1928, the small bundle which made a reluctant and silent entry into a world, blighted by hate, later resolved to enrich himself with words, so strong and powerful, that even his peers in schools were browbeaten. These words then went on to talk of the redemptive power of truth and non-violence, becoming beacon lights to guide humanity towards a better world. It is due to his colossal efforts, that the African-Americans were able to rid themselves of emasculating captivity – socially, financially, politically and psychologically. When he dreamt, his brethren dreamt along with him. When he thundered, they added their own roars to the thunder.

'*Get on your walking shoes, walk together, children, and don't cha get weary*,' King exhorted the audience of over a thousand at Shiloh Baptist Church in Albany on 15 December 1961, and they walked together, untired and singing '*we shall overcome*'.

When his words were orphaned on 4 April 1968, his brethren felt orphaned too. What he proclaimed in 1959, after his highly satisfying visit to India still rings true: '*We have a power, power that can't be found in Molotov cocktails, but we do have a power. Power that cannot be found in bullets and guns, but we have a power.'* And now, as we hear the ear-callousing cacophony of hatred all around us, his words ring loud and clear: *Over the bleached bones and jumbled residues of civilisations are written the words 'too late'.* Let us not find ourselves in the pathetic condition of wringing our hands, and lamenting too late, too late!

On 18 March 2008, Senator Barack Obama had delivered a 40-minute speech in Philadelphia, emphasising the document that the founding fathers produced at the Philadelphia Convention 221 years ago was '*ultimately unfinished. It was stained by this nation's original sin of slavery ...*'

> '...words on parchment would not be enough to deliver slaves from bondage or provide men and women of every colour and creed their full rights and obligations as citizens of the United States. What would be needed were Americans in successive generations who were willing to do their part – through protests and struggles...to narrow the gap between the promise of our ideals and the reality of their time.'

Exactly 45 years after King's powerful baritone talked of his '*dream*' of inclusiveness, 47-year-old Barack Obama became the 44th president of USA on 20 January 2009.

When he was elected US President on 4 November 2008, he became the first African-American to adorn the White House. Had King's dream finally taken tangible shape? Or were the contours just hazy? His election was indeed an incredibly emotional moment for all blacks. With glowing faces, straightened backs, and proud voices, they could finally tell their children and grandchildren, that they had finally overcome, really and truly. With an African-American at the helm, they could dream anew, of moving *'in the same direction – towards a better future for our children and grandchildren'*.

Slowly, but steadily, despite the authorities' emphasis on gradualism, they had really marched forward, hand in resilient hand, on the road to inclusiveness, fair play, equality and justice. With Obama's election, the dream had irrevocably shifted from the realm of an impossibility into the realm of concrete possibility. The centennial injustice and disparity could not, however, be set right by one stroke of the pen but it was indeed an edifying moment, a moment of triumph.

Although, the blacks have made long and powerful strides towards the realisation of King's dream, the struggle has to continue and much remains to be overcome, till justice becomes *'a reality for all God's children'*.

New York Times, 3 April 2018

As the US prepared to commemorate the 50th anniversary of King's assassination on 4 April 2018, Rev Jesse Jackson, founder and president of the Rainbow PUSH Coalition, a former aide to Rev Dr Martin Luther King Jr who happened to be one of the few people with him in his last moments, spoke thus:

> *'While danger was all around, we never thought the Martin Luther King we knew and loved, admitted to Morehouse College at 15, graduated and ordained at 19, earning a PhD at 26, awarded the Nobel Peace Prize at 35, would be dead at 39.'*

He further stated:

> 'He led the Montgomery bus boycott and navigated police terror in Birmingham. He got us over the bloodstained bridge in Selma and survived the rocks and bottles and hatred in Chicago. He globalised our struggle to end the war in Vietnam.
> How he lived is why he died.
> We are in a battle for the soul of America, and it's not enough to admire Dr King. To admire him is to reduce him to a mere celebrity. It requires no commitment, no action. Those who value justice and equality must have the will and courage to follow him. They must be ready to sacrifice.'

'A man of peace, he died violently. A man of love, he died hated by many,' said the *New York Times*.

> 'Dr King's spirit has been our moral guidepost for 50 years. That spirit is alive today with the high school students of Parkland, Fla., as they push the country toward sensible gun control. It is alive with the teachers of West Virginia, who have blazed a trail for other workers. It is alive with

> Black Lives Matter, the Dreamers, Colin Kaepernick and thousands of African-American voters who defied the pundits and sent an Alabama Democrat to the Senate for the first time in a generation. It is alive with the Rev William Barber as he resurrects Dr King's last crusade, the Poor People's Campaign.'

We should not forget that he was definitely not someone who had attained sainthood, but a man not without human frailties, vulnerabilities and fears, who reiterated many a time that everyone has two sides to one's character; the good and the evil were always dueling inside a person's body; the higher and the lower selves were always at loggerheads. Saddled with an enormous conscience, even against heavy odds, he had always tried his best to keep the higher self in command.

If he had been alive in this spiritually bankrupt world, his impassioned baritone would once again appeal to America to stop the insanity of violence, pleading with America to pull its troops out of Syria to redeem its soul. At the massacre of innocent civilians and children in Syria, his heart would have bled, his love-drenched voice would have once again risen above the cacophony of bigotry, hate, violence, anguish and fear: a voice that broke its silence over the Vietnam War on 4 April 1967 at the Riverside Church, in New York:

> *'Over the bleached bones and jumbled residues of numerous civilisations are written the pathetic words "too late", we still have a choice today; non-violent coexistence or violent co-annihilation.'*

This hate-filled world would once again echo with his rumbling eloquence and persuasive conviction, beseeching it to put an end to '*revenge, aggression and retaliation*', making place for the reign of love, for never were we more deeply '*in need of a new way, beyond the darkness that seems so close around us*'.

So, it is the crying need of the hour to rededicate ourselves, as King wanted so many years back, to the struggle for a new world, bursting with love, compassion, sincerity, non-violence, harmony and peace.

King's Mentors

Henry David Thoreau

Gandhi

Benjamin Elijah Mays

Edgar Sheffield Brightman

Walter Rauschenbusch

Gladstone Lewis

Friends in Civil Rights movement

Andrew Young

Bernard Lee

Hosea Williams

Chauncey Eskridge (C)

Rabbi Heschel

James Lawson

Ralph Abernathy

Reference

THE EARLY YEARS

1. King, A., 18 January 1973, *Martin Luther King Jr: Birth To Twelve Years Old*, Ebenezer Baptist Church, King Centre Recording, p 41
2. King, M. L. Jr, & Clayborne, C. (Ed), 1998, *The Autobiography of Martin Luther King Jr*, Warner Books, p 6
3. Ibid, p 5
4. Ibid, p 1

MOREHOUSE COLLEGE

1. King, M. L. Jr & Clayborne, C. (Ed.), 1998, *The Autobiography of Martin Luther Jr*, Warner Books, Chapter 2.
2. Ibid.
3. Schulke, F. & Mcphee P.O. 1986, *King Remembered,* Pocket books, New York, p 14.
4. Oates, S. B., 1985, *Let the Trumpet Sound,* A mentor Book, USA, p 18.
5. Mays, B. E., 1971, *Born to Rebel,* Charles Scribner's Sons,

New York, p 196.

6. Schulke, F. & Mcphee, P. O., 1986, *King Remembered,* Pocket books, New York, p 16.
7. Downing, F. L., 1986, *To See the Promised Land: The Faith Pilgrimage of Martin Luther King Jr,* Mercer University Press, Atlanta, p 137.
8. Long, M. G, 2002, *Against Us but For Us: Martin Luther Jr, and the State,* Georgia, p 29.
9. Ibid, p 30.
10. King, M. L. Jr & Clayborne C. (Ed), *The Autobiography of Martin Luther Jr,* Warner Books, p 1.
11. King, M. L. Jr, 1958, *Stride toward Freedom,* Harper & Row Publishers, p 91

AT CROZER SEMINARY

1. King, M. L. Jr & Clayborne, C. (Ed), 1998, *The Autobiography of Martin Luther King Jr*, Warner Books, Chapter 3.
2. Frazier, L. E., 2012, *King: A False Prophet?*, Lulu Press Inc.

KING AT BOSTON UNIVERSITY

1. Roberts, J. D., 2005: *Bonhoeffer and King: Speaking Truth to Power,* Westminster John Knok Press, Louisville, p 37.
2. Ibid, p 39.
3. Ibid, p 40.
4. Steinkraus, W. E., 1973, *Martin Luther King's Personalism, and Non-violence,* Journal of the History

of Ideas, *Vol. 34, No. 1,* (January–March 1973), Univ. of Pennsylvania Press, p 97–111.

5. King, M. L. Jr & Clayborne, C. (Ed), 1998, *The autobiography of Martin Luther King Jr*, Warner Books, Chapter 4.
6. Born on 27 April 1927, Coretta graduated in Music from Antioch College in Yellow Springs, Ohio. In 1951, she enrolled at the New England Conservatory of Music earning a degree in voice and violin.

   Known as 'the first lady of the Civil rights movement', President George Bush in his State of the Union address called her, 'beloved, graceful and courageous.' After Martin's death, she continued to work for the promotion of her husband's legacy of equality, peace, justice and non-violence. She created the Martin Luther King Jr Center for non-violent social change in 1968, and co-founded many other organisations, such as the *Black Leadership Forum* and the *Black Leadership Roundtable.* She travelled throughout the world making speeches against social injustice.

   Just a few days after Martin's assassination, Coretta led a March on behalf of sanitation workers in Memphsis and, in the same month, she kept Martin's speaking engagement at an anti-Vietnam rally in New York. In May 1968, she helped the launching of the March on Washington of the Poor Peoples' campaign and participated in anti-poverty efforts.

   On 16 August 2005, Coretta King suffered a paralysing stroke and a mild heart attack. On 31 January 2006, she passed away at the age of 78, at Mexico, where she had gone to consult physicians regarding treatment for her ovarian cancer.

Coretta was a lifelong admirer of Gandhi ever since her visit to India in 1959. She described Gandhi as Martin's 'political mentor'. She wholeheartedly supported the projects of peace and non-violence, as preached by Gandhi and Martin, and tried to keep the spirit of both apostles of non-violence alive.

7. She was only 12-year old when her father was assassinated in 1968, Alabama. An actress, producer, author, a motivational speaker, she died in May 2007, at the age of 51, in Santa Monica, California.
8. Schulke, F. & Mcphee, P. O., 1986, *King Remembered,* Pocket books, New York, p 31.

Bibliography

Ansbro, John J. Martin Luther King, Jr: Nonviolent Strategies and Tactics for Social Change, Madison Books, 2000

Ansbro, John J Martin Luther King Jr, The Making of a Mind, Orbis Books, 1984

Baldwin, Lewis. Never to Leave Us Alone: The Prayer Life of Martin Luther King Jr Fortress Press, 2010

Baldwin, Lewis. There is a Balm in Gilead. Fortress Press, 1991

Baldwin, Lewis. To Make the Wounded Whole. 1992. Fortress Press Bennett

Brinkley, Douglas, Rosa Parks, Viking, New York, 2000

Bennett, Lerone, Jr What Manner of Man. Chicago: Johnson Publishing Co., Book Division, 1964

Bennett, Lerone Jr Before the Mayflower: A History of Black America. New York: Viking Penguin, 1984

Clayborne Carson [ed.] King, Martin Luther, Jr The Autobiography of Martin Luther King Jr New York: Intellectual Properties Management, 1998 in association with Warner Books, USA'

Dan R Warren : If It Takes All Summer: Martin Luther King, the KKK, and States' Rights in St Augustine, 1964 University of Alabama Press, 2008

David L Chappell, A Stone of Hope, Chapel Hill: University of North Carolina Press, 2004

Downing, Frederick L. To see the Promised Land: The Faith Pilgrimage of Martin Luther King Jr, Mercer University Press, 1986

Eddie S. Glaude Jr, Democracy in Black: How race still enslaves in America, Crown, 2016

Ellison, Ralph, Invisible Man, Random House, New York, 1952

Farmer, James. Lay Bare the Heart. New York: Arbor House, 1985

Fairclough, Adam. Martin Luther King, Jr Athens: University of Georgia Press, 1995.

Frady, Marshall. Martin Luther King, Jr New York: Penguin Group, 2002

Fager, Charles E., Selma 1965: The March that Changed the South. Boston: Beacon Press, 1985

Fairclough, Adam: To Redeem the Soul of America: The SCLC and Martin Luther King, Jr Athens: University of Georgia, 1987

Farmer, James. Lay Bare the Heart. New York: Arbor House, 1985

Garrow, David J, MLK: An American Legacy: Open Road Media, 2016:

-Bearing the Cross

- Protest at Selma

- The FBI and Martin Luther King Jr

Gilliard, Deric A. Unsung: Living in the Shadows of a Legend: Unsung Heroes and Sheroes Who Marched With Dr Martin Luther King, Jr Gilliard Communications. 2002

Harding, Vincent. Martin Luther King: The Inconvenient Hero. Orbis Books. 1996

Jackson, Thomas F From Civil Rights to Human Rights: Martin Luther King, Jr and the Struggle for Economic Justice (Politics and Culture in Modern America). University of Pennsylvania Press, 2009

James Echols -I Have a Dream: Martin Luther King Jr and the Future of Multicultural America , Fortress Press, 2004

James R Ralph Jr: Northern Protest: Martin Luther King, Jr, Chicago, and the Civil Rights Movement , Harvard University Press, 1993

John A Kirk, Martin Luther King Jr Pearson Longman, 2005

Jeanne, Theoharis: The Rebellious life of Mrs Rosa Parks, Thorndike Maine, 2013

Jackson Troy: Becoming King: Martin Luther King, Jr and the Making of a National Leader, University Press of Kentucky, 2008

Jonathan Reider, Gospel of Freedom: Martin Luther King Jr's Letter from Birmingham Jail and the struggle that changed a nation, Bloomsbury Press, New York, 2013

King, Coretta Scott. My Life with Martin Luther King, Jr New York: Holt, Rinehart and Winston, 1969

King, Coretta Scott, [Ed.]. The Words of Martin Luther King Jr New York: New market Press, 1983

King, Farris, Christine: Through it all: Reflections on my life, my family and my Faith, Atria Books, January, 2001

King, Farris, Christine, My Brother Martin: A sister remembers growing up with the Rev. Dr Martin Luther King Jr; Baker and Taylor, 2009

King, Dexter Scott. Growing Up King: An Intimate Memoir: Grand Central Publishing, 2003

King, Rev. Martin Luther, Sr Daddy King: An Autobiography. New York: William Morrow & Co. Inc., 1980

Leventhal, Willy S.: The Children Coming on: A Retrospective of the Montgomery Bus Boycott. Black Belt Press. 1998

Lewis, John. Walking with the Wind: A Memoir of the Movement. Mariner Books. 1999

Lerone Jr Before the Mayflower: A History of Black America. New York: Viking Penguin, 1984

Lincoln C Eric [Ed.] Martin Luther King Jr: A Profile, Hill & Wang, New York, 1970

Michelle Alexander: The new Jim Crow, New Press, 2012

Millender, Dharathula H. Martin Luther King Jr: Young man with a dream. Indianapolis: Bobbs-Merrill, 1983

Moses, Greg. Revolution of Conscience: Martin Luther King, Jr and the Philosophy of Nonviolence. The Guilford Press, 1998

Michael J Nojeim: Gandhi and King: The Power of Nonviolent Resistance Praeger, USA 2004

Moses, Greg. Revolution of Conscience: Martin Luther King, Jr and the Philosophy of Nonviolence. The Guilford Press

Pepper, William F. Orders to Kill: The Truth Behind the Murder of Martin Luther King, Jr New York: IPM in Association with Warner Books, 1995

Philips, Donald T. Martin Luther King, Jr On Leadership. New

York: Warner Books, 1999

Richard Wayne Willis Sr Martin Luther King, Jr and the Image of God Oxford University Press, 2009

Morris, Aldon. The Origins of the Civil Rights Movement. New York: Free Press, 1984

Pickering, George W., and Alan B. Anderson. Confronting the Color Line: Broken Promise of the Civil Rights Movement in Chicago. Athens: University of Georgia, 1986

Raines, Howell. My Soul Is Rested. New York: Viking Penguin, 1977

Robinson, JoAnn. The Montgomery Bus Boycott and the Women Who Started It: The Memoir of JoAnn Gibson Robinson. Knoxville: University of Tennessee Press, 1987

Schulke F and Mc Phee Penelope, King Remembered, Pocket Books, New York, 1986

Oates, Stephen B. Let the Trumpet Sound, A Mentor Book, Penguin 1985

Williams, Juan. Eyes on the Prize: America's Civil Rights Years, 1954-1965. New York: Viking, 1987.

Witherspoon, Wm. Roger. Martin Luther King, Jr: To the Mountaintop. Garden City: Doubleday & Co., Inc., 1985

Watkins, Angela Farris. My Uncle Martin's Big Heart: Abrams Books for Young Readers

Yanco Jennifer J ,Misremembering Dr King: Revisiting the Legacy of Martin Luther King Jr Jennifer Indiana University Press, 2014

Yeboah Samuel, Kennedy, 'The Ideology of Racism, Hansib Publishing, England, 1988

Young, Andrew. An Easy Burden: The Civil Rights Movement

and the Transformation of America. Baylor Press. 2008

Young, Andrew. A Way Out of No Way; the Spiritual Memoirs of Andrew Young. Thomas Nelson, Inc. 1996

BOOKS BY MARTIN LUTHER KING Jr:

Strength to Love. New York: Harper & Row Publishers, 1963

Stride toward Freedom: The Montgomery Story. New York: Harper & Row Publishers, 1958

The Trumpet of Conscience. New York: Harper & Row Publishers, 1968. (Foreword by Coretta Scott King.)

Where Do We Go From Here: Chaos or Community? New York: Harper & Row Publishers, 1967

Why We Can't Wait. New York: Harper & Row Publishers, 1963

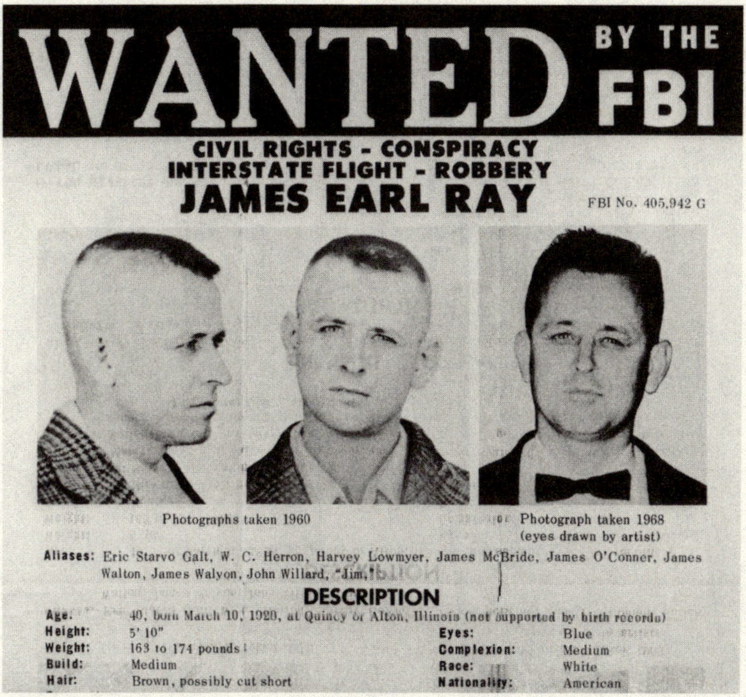

King died at the hospital but his assassin, a man called Ray, escaped and was captured two months later in the United Kingdom. James Earl Ray was a fugitive from the Missouri State Penitentiary. He was arrested on 8 June 1968, in London at Heathrow Airport, extradited to the United States, and charged with the crime. On 10 March 1969, he pleaded guilty and was sentenced to 99 years in the Tennessee State Penitentiary. He died in prison in 1998.

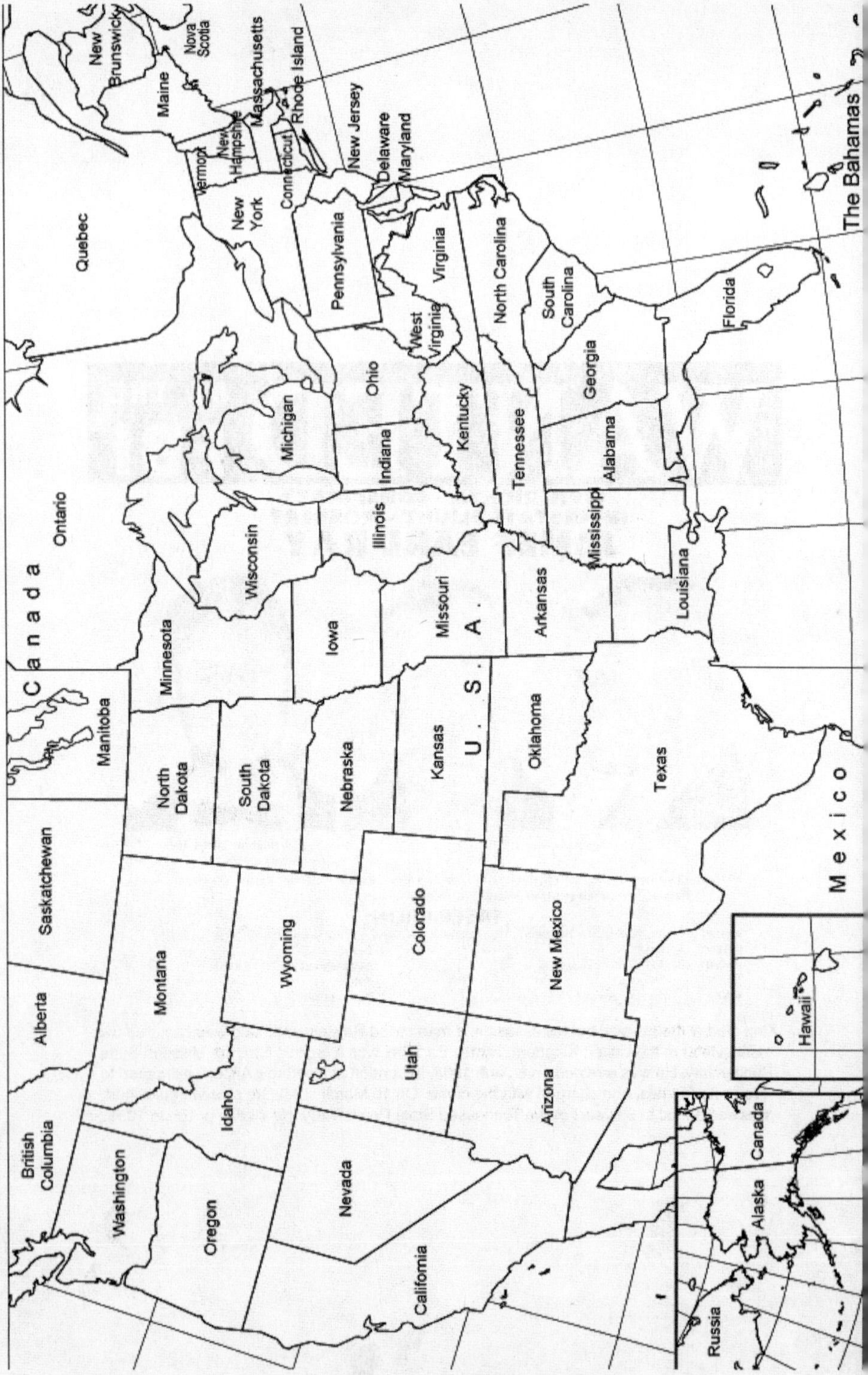

Representational Map of the USA: Not to scale